MISSIONAL
HOUSE
CHURCHES

Reaching Our Communities with the Gospel

J. D. PAYNE

Paternoster:
thinking faith

COLORADO SPRINGS · MILTON KEYNES · HYDERABAD

Paternoster Publishing
We welcome your questions and comments.

USA   1820 Jet Stream Drive, Colorado Springs, CO 80921
       www.authenticbooks.com
UK   9 Holdom Avenue, Bletchley, Milton Keynes, Bucks, MK1 1QR
       www.authenticmedia.co.uk
India Logos Bhavan, Medchal Road, Jeedimetla Village, Secunderabad
       500 055, A.P.

Missional House Churches
ISBN-13: 978-1-934068-25-0
ISBN-10: 1-934068-25-X

Cover and interior design: projectluz.com
Editorial team: Bette Smyth, Dana Bromley

Printed in the United States of America

MISSIONAL HOUSE CHURCHES

Contents

To my heavenly Lord,
who builds his church,

and

to my earthly partner,
Sarah, the greatest wife
and mother.

Acknowledgments

As I write this section of this book, I do so with great fear that I will most definitely forget someone who is worthy of mention. I get the feeling that I am like a Grammy or Oscar winner standing on stage stammering and stuttering, surprised that I am receiving an award and fearful of forgetting to say thanks to someone.

First and foremost, I must thank the Lord Jesus for allowing me to have the vision and ability to complete this work. Though this book is certainly not perfect, I am thankful that he allowed me to do the research and share my findings about what is happening in a largely unfamiliar segment of the body of Christ.

Several years ago, I committed my life to follow Jesus, who died for the sins of the world and offers salvation to all. It is not always the easiest way of life, but I strongly urge you to follow him who alone offers abundant and eternal life. He receives all who will turn from their sinful ways and confess him as Lord, believing that God raised him from the dead (see Romans 10:9).

Though I am just an author, he is the Author of all life and greatly desires that your story be a part of his story.

Some researchers have a budget for research projects; I did not. Whether it was measured in dollars, euros, rupees, or pounds, my budget was the same in any currency: zilch. Despite this limitation, I believe the work in your hands did not suffer too substantially. It is my hope that the limitations of my study will be the catalyst for more and better research on house churches.

Though I did not have the luxury of highly skilled researchers, I was greatly blessed to have two students who volunteered their time to work with me. Sam Dyer and Dan Rice are two great guys with servant hearts. They spent several hours conducting interviews and meeting with me. I owe a debt of gratitude to these two men and their assistance. Thank you guys!

I also must thank Kathy Webb and Kari Plevan, two secretaries with whom I have had the privilege to work with throughout the course of my research and publication of this work. Thank you, ladies, for your Christ-like spirits and assistance with this work.

A special thanks goes to Susan Wilder for her assistance with developing my on-line survey tool and collecting the data.

There were several friends who read and commented on various versions of this work long before it went to the publisher. Al James offered numerous outstanding comments and suggestions. My dean, Chuck Lawless, also provided a great amount of guidance and wisdom. Thank you, Al and Chuck, for going above and beyond the call of duty.

Daniel Sanchez, Gary Smith, David Sills, George Garner, Mark Terry, Joe Richard, and Felicity Dale read early drafts and provided great insights and suggestions. I thank all of you for your assistance with my first book.

I first met Elmer Towns during the summer of 2006 at a meeting where he was a guest speaker. After obtaining a copy of my manuscript on that same day, he read the entire draft overnight and provided me with immediate, substantive feedback. Thank you, Dr. Towns, for your generous contribution in spite of your demanding schedule.

Two of the most influential individuals in many house church circles today are Tony Dale and Neil Cole. These two men assisted me in locating participants for the research on which this book's contents are based. Thank you, men, for you contribution to this material.

A special word of thanks is in order to those survey participants who gave their time to answer numerous survey questions. Unless permission was specifically granted, as a researcher, I provided all participants with confidentiality. Though you will not come to know the church leaders by name, you will get a better understanding of the churches they serve. Without these participants, this book could not have been written.

The folks at Authentic Publishing have been a great blessing with whom to work. I greatly appreciate the relationship that I have developed with Volney James. Thanks, Volney, for being willing to work with me on my first book. Thank you Angela Lewis, Dana Carrington, and Bette Smyth for all of your work as well.

Much appreciation is due to the members of the Payne household. Without them, this book would not have been what it is today; without them, I would not be who I am today. Thank you Sarah, Hannah, Rachel, and Joel. I love you very much.

Though there are many people who contributed to this

work in some fashion or another, I take full ownership for the contents. Any shortcomings of this work are to be charged to my account and none to the aforementioned individuals.

Introduction

Interest in house churches in general and those in North America in particular has been growing over the past several years. A Google search of the words *house church* reveals over one million results. Numerous books discussing house churches have been written in the last thirty years.[1] Since I started writing this book, I have already seen two stories on North American house churches on national news television programs[2] and read one story in *Time* magazine[3] and another in a Lexington, Kentucky,[4] newspaper and I was not even searching for such stories. Just this past week, a friend sent me an article noting that perhaps one in five North American adults attend a house church at least once a month.[5] As we continue into the twenty-first century, interest in and growth of such churches will likely continue.

The Bible is very clear that the apostolic Church met in homes. Upon returning from the Mount of Ascension, the believers prayed together in an upper room (Acts 1:12–14). On the day of Pentecost, the believers were gathered in a house when the Spirit fell on them (Acts 2:2). After the baptism of the three thousand, the believers not only met in the temple court but they also met in houses (Acts 2:46). It is no wonder that Luke later uses the expression "house after house" to describe the environments in which Saul made his arrests (Acts 8:3); the house was a common place to find believers.[6]

Even in Thessalonica, the jealous Jews led a mob to Jason's house to arrest Paul and Silas (Acts 17:5). When Peter was arrested, the church gathered in Mary's house for prayer (Acts 12:12). In his Miletus address to the Ephesian elders, Paul reminded them of his practice of teaching in "public and from house to house" (Acts 20:20). In his Colossian letter, Paul sent his greetings to "Nympha and the church in her house" (Colossians 4:15). Paul also sent his greetings to the church meeting in Philemon's house (Philemon 1). Concluding his Roman correspondence, Paul sent greetings to the church meeting in the home of Priscilla and Aquila (Romans 16:5).[7]

This book is the result of researching thirty-three evangelistic house churches. The primary purpose for writing this work is to describe what is taking place among these churches that are both baptizing recent converts and planting other churches. Though much of this work is descriptive, there are several corollaries that follow.

First, I'm interested in the biblical tradition of meeting in homes that continues today. Following the days of the apostolic Church, churches continued to meet in houses, even after Constantine made Christianity an official religion in AD 313 with the Edict of Milan.[8] Two thousand years of Church history point to the fact that what I am writing about is nothing new.

Second, I incorporate my own experiences into this writing. Though I have been involved in a variety of cultural expressions of the Church over the years, two years of my life were spent ministering in a house church.

The reader should know I am traditional to the core and very thankful for and proud of my heritage. I am a fourth-generation Southern Baptist and strongly support my denomination through my current local church, through serving as a national missionary with the North American Mission Board, and by teaching at the Southern Baptist Theological Seminary. Some of my earliest memories of church life are driving on Sunday mornings down an old, gravel southeastern Kentucky country road to a rustic building where a small congregation gathered for study and worship. I came to faith in Christ and felt the Lord leading me into pastoral ministry when I was a part of a larger church, yet one very traditional in form, function, and style. I started my preaching ministry over fourteen years ago in many small rural congregations. I preached one of my first sermons from a pulpit in a small country church that did not even have plumbing. For several years, I pastored small traditional churches. *Please understand*, I have many wonderful experiences and memories in traditional church life. I love the traditional church, *and I do not write this book to belittle, degrade, or discard the traditional established local church.* Every year I preach to, equip, encourage, and partner with numerous traditional churches for the sake of the gospel. Much of my time each day is spent building up and supporting the body of Christ as it is expressed in traditional ways.

This is not a book on how to "fix" the traditional church. Neither is this a book on how to lead a traditional church to become a house church. This is not a book attempting to destroy traditional church cultures. This book is not a prescription for "how to do church," but rather this work is *primarily* a description of what is a present reality in the United States.

As a researcher, I know that a fine line exists between describing the findings and advocating and critiquing the practices discovered. All researchers have some biases. Though my writing is primarily based on exploratory research and is descriptive in nature, there will be times throughout this book when I will advocate for what I believe is healthy theology and healthy local church practices revealed in the findings. However, on other occasions, I will share my concerns regarding what I believe to be problematic beliefs and practices of some house churches.

This book is not a declaration that the house church model is the only proper expression of the body of Christ or the answer to the Church's problems. In North America today, unfortunately, we are infatuated with models and methods. We travel the continent and spend great amounts of time and money looking for cutting-edge and innovative ways of how to do church. I agree with Neil Cole who said, "The answers are not found in our models, methods, and manmade systems but in the truth of God's Word and in being filled and led by the Spirit of God."[9]

This book is not a description or critique of the contemporary House Church Movement taking place in the United States and Canada. Just as all growing churches of the 1980s and 1990s did not consider themselves part of the Church Growth Movement, not all house churches consider themselves to be a part of the House Church Movement. Though it is possible that some of the churches in our study would consider themselves to be a part of this movement, our survey did not inquire into this matter.

There is a theological reason for writing this book. In general, the North American Church in all of its expressions is facing an ecclesiological identity crisis. Also, as a missiologist who trains church planters, I believe that the most critical issue in North American church planting is an ecclesiological issue. We struggle in answering the question, What is the Church? This crisis has caused me to offer a biblical critique of the ecclesiological concerns that were specifically derived from my house church research, my pastoral experience, and my personal observations over the last several years.

The body of Christ should always be concerned when local churches, whatever their cultural expression (for example, house, purpose-driven, traditional), manifest ungodly standards and practices. When churches believe in the classical doctrines of orthodox Christianity and do things well, however, we should be thankful and look to them as examples of those contending for the faith that was once for all delivered to the saints (Jude 3).

A few years ago, my wife and I decided to finish hanging sheetrock in our garage. Unfortunately, we lacked the most basic carpentry skills. After I knocked several holes in the sheetrock in my attempt to drive nails, I was forced to do the necessary patch-work. No matter how hard I tried to make the wallboard look smooth and finished, the marred surface was obvious. Standing in our garage, away from the wall, my eyes were naturally drawn to the numerous blemishes from my mighty hammer.

Just as several blemishes on my garage wall caused the observer to miss the areas of good work, in a similar way, many churches have gained attention as being biblically errant in their practices and are the ones most people consider when they hear the expression *house church*. For example, some churches have rejected pastoral leadership, become isolated from the larger body of Christ, become inwardly focused, and discarded the value of the Word of God.

My desire is to report on those churches that *appear* to manifest historically orthodox beliefs and practices. Please realize, you and I may not agree completely with their philosophies, methods, structures, and organizations, but our disagreement does not automatically make them heretics. As a Baptist, I may not agree with the Presbyterian Church when it practices infant baptism, but I am not going to blackball all Presbyterians. Just as all traditional churches are not standardized in their convictions and practices, likewise, all house churches are not standardized in their convictions and practices.

I also write this book to reveal what is going on among those churches that are making disciples. This focus separates this book from other books on house churches. As of the present, we have undertaken the largest study of North American evangelistic house churches.[10] This book contains the findings from our study.

It is also my desire to stimulate conversation. If you read this book and have several unanswered questions, then I have accomplished one of my goals. More Christ-glorifying research, critique, and discussion on house churches needs to occur in North America. This is a field ripe for dialogue. It is an expression of the body of Christ that the North American twenty-first century Church must address. To help stimulate additional research, I will confess the limitations of this study when appropriate. I will also make suggestions to assist future researchers in developing better survey tools.

Finally, when we examine the growth of the Church outside of the West, we see that simple expressions of church life are commonplace. A plethora of examples can be cited from most continents of church planting movements where the gospel is spreading rapidly while churches are being planted exponentially. I write to discuss the potential of rapid church growth and multiplication in the Western world. Recently, George Barna commented that house churches are one of the fastest growing models of churches.[11] For several years I have wondered what church planting movements would look like if they occurred in the West. The United States has no church planting movements. If they do occur, many of the churches represented in this book are likely positioned to play a significant role in catalyzing such simple, rapid, and reproducible movements.

WHAT'S IN A LABEL?

Though I am one of the 44.6 million U.S. citizens who comprise Generation X, I do not have a label phobia like some of my generation. Labels give us an ideal-type on which we compare present and future information. For example, my study of jazz music helps me understand when someone says a band has a 'big band' sound. We need labels; they help us identify and explain concepts. Labels are not always bad. With this understanding of labels, I'll explain my use of certain words.

CHURCH AND CHURCH

Throughout this book, when I use the word *Church* with an uppercase *C*, I am speaking of the universal body of Christ, a denomination, or the entire body of Christ on a particular continent (for example, North American Church). The word *church* with a lowercase *c* refers to the local expression of the body of Christ, a local church. Throughout the New Testament, both of these expressions of the body of Christ (that is, universal and local) are taught.[12] At times, I refer to both the universal and the local church. If the distinction cannot be determined from the context, I use "C/church" when referring to both.

Recently, my denomination has thoroughly discussed this issue.[13] A local church is comprised of a regenerate and baptized membership. In its covenant identity, essence, and practice, these believers are an autonomous local body of Christ. Under the guidance of the Holy Spirit and God's Word, they are self-supporting, self-governing, and self-propagating. They are kingdom citizens living according to a kingdom ethic in covenant community with one another.

Though a group of believers may gather together for a Bible study or a time of worship, neither their regenerate nature nor their function alone make them a local church. They are obviously part of the universal (invisible) Church, but they are not necessarily a local church.

Missional Church

I use the term *missional*[14] to distinguish house churches that engage the culture with the gospel, make disciples, and plant churches from those house churches that do not. A missional church is not content to talk about the need to do missions, to have missions as a separate program within the congregation, or to understand missions as something done two weeks every summer or on Thursday nights at the homeless shelter. A missional church is evangelistic not simply because a gospel invitation is given at the end of their Sunday gatherings or because it has a community visitation program on Tuesday nights. Missional churches have within their very DNA a passion to take the gospel to their Jerusalem, Judea, and Samaria, and throughout the world. They believe if they cease to be intentionally and regularly involved in evangelism, then they cease to be a church.

Missional churches obey our Lord's command to "go" into all the world rather than waiting for unbelievers to come to their church gatherings.

A caveat needs to be made. I recognize there are serious limitations to my definition of missional house churches. I confess that I use the term *missional* quite loosely. Also, I do not mean to imply that the only missional churches are the house churches in our study.

Our parameters of what constitutes a missional house church were simply two-fold. First, they had to have baptized at least one person within the previous year of the study. Second, they had to have planted at least one congregation within the past three years. Many churches in North America do not baptize a single person in a given year. For example, in the Southern Baptist Convention (SBC) in 2003, 13,465 churches (31.3 percent of SBC churches) did not baptize anyone.[15] Therefore, I set our research parameter very low. Though baptisms do not necessarily mean that conversions are happening, they are a fairly reliable indicator of conversion growth.

Also, because few churches in North America are involved in church planting, I set the other parameter low. The churches in our study had to have planted at least one church in the previous three years. Though church planting does not guarantee that evangelism is occurring, it usually shows that an outward focus is present.

HOUSE CHURCH

Though the label *house* is necessary for research and reporting, unfortunately, the label conveys the notion that there is "church" and then there is "house church," implying that one expression is more legitimate than the other or that there are different degrees of church. In no way am I attempting to communicate that one cultural expression of the body is the only genuine expression. Though the churches represented in our study met in houses most of the time, their identity as a church was not derived from their meeting place. They were the local expression of the body of Christ whether they met in a house, a park, or a conference hall. Many leaders in these churches would identify with Steve Atkerson's words, "'House church' is just a convenient label to describe a whole range of topics about the church and how it should function."[16] However, none of the churches in our study had a problem referring to themselves as "house churches."[17] Because of this self-designated appellation, I will refer to these churches as house churches and will address their uniqueness in the following chapters.

Traditional Church

Throughout this book, I frequently speak of the *traditional* or *mainstream* local church. This label is also a necessary problem for research and reporting. Hopefully, future researchers will resolve the challenge with the use of such labels. By using this label, I am not saying that all churches that are not house churches are the same, neither am I attempting to polarize churches that are "house" and churches that are "traditional." I have a difficult time using this label. The reason for such a label is to offer a point of reference, or a type, whereby the reader can attempt to gain a grasp of the difference between the churches in this book and the overwhelming majority (that is, mainstream) of churches that comprise the North American ecclesiological landscape.

In this study "traditional" describes the generally held understanding of the local church. Traditional churches usually have

Sunday morning as their primary time to gather. The Sunday worship gathering generally requires much time and energy to prepare for a one- or two-hour weekly event. For many such churches, the majority of their income is devoted to ministers' salaries and physical properties. These churches tend to be campus-based in their identities. It is at these locations that the majority of their ministry events occur.

Traditional churches tend to be program-oriented, event-oriented, or categorically purpose-oriented in their identities. Pastoral leadership tends to be more positional in orientation and less relational. Evangelism is, many times, one program among many programs of the church and/or is primarily accomplished through the members inviting unbelievers to a worship service where the gospel is shared. The number of members usually far exceeds the number of people who gather weekly for worship and actively use their gifts and talents to build up the church. Many traditional churches identify themselves primarily in terms of their services, events, structures, buildings, and organizations.

HOUSE CHURCHES IN NORTH AMERICA

House churches in the West are not new. In fact, the first Western church met in the house of a wealthy merchant named Lydia (Acts 16:15, 40). Wolfgang Simpson reminds us that most western churches begin as house churches: "Almost all contemporary church-plants in the West go through an organic house-church phase in their early days. Many Western Christians still look back with fond memories of the spontaneous early months or the 'good old times when we still had our church in homes.' The problem is not so much that there are no house churches in the West but that this form of church has neither been consciously acknowledged nor actively sought after."[18]

Also, Jack Redford, former director of church extension with the Home Mission Board (now North American Mission Board) of the SBC, noted that in the 1970s, establishing a mission fellowship (the church in embryonic form) was a necessary step toward constituting a new church. Though Redford later discussed the construction of buildings for new congregations, he noted that in the early days of the church planting work "the meeting place can be almost anywhere, but the home is the most satisfactory place in most cases."[19]

Larry Kreider notes that Mike Steele, who oversees DAWN (Discipling a Whole Nation) in North America, has been monitoring the growth of house churches on this continent. According to Steele,

> House church networks are springing up around the country. Some have been going for a long time; others are just being birthed and some are only a few years old. The Foursquare church has a house church planting team in Canada. The Baptists in Texas have a network of five house churches in the Dallas area. Dallas has several folks spreading house churches across the city. There are house church networks emerging in Ames, Iowa, and Billings, Montana. One of my dear friends is leading a fellowship of home churches in Denver. They are currently meeting in four homes that soon will expand to nine. There is a house church network in Portland, Oregon, for over a decade. There are others meeting in Salem, Oregon. In Austin, Texas, there is a thriving house church network that is linking with house church

networks in San Antonio and Dallas. In Houston,
one of my good friends has a network of four house
churches. They reach into the youth culture. There
is a group from the San Francisco Bay area planting
house churches in that city and a group of young
people in Northern California planting 25 house
churches.[20]

Though I have yet to see clear evidence of the actual number
of house churches in North America, some have made an attempt
to estimate their number. These estimates are not very helpful
since there is much discrepancy between them. According to
Laurie Goodstein's article in *The New York Times,* as many as
1,600 groups in all fifty states are listed on various websites.[21]
Citing Rick Hiebert's article, "There's No Church Like Home,"
Rad Zdero states, "It has been estimated that there are about
200 house churches in Canada and about 1500 in the United
States."[22] Citing a much greater estimate, Rita Healy and David
Van Biema note that some have set the number from 50,000
into the millions.[23]

House Churches or Cell Churches?

Due to the growing popularity of cell churches in the
United States, a common question today is, What is the difference between house churches and cell churches? The general
answer revolves around the two issues of autonomy and pastoral
leadership. Though a house church may be small in membership
(this is not always the case), it considers itself fully autonomous,
meaning that, under the headship of Christ and the Word,
the church makes its own decisions regarding plans, strategies,
purchases, leadership, worship expressions, missions, and so on.

No overarching authoritative body or board dictates to the local congregation what the church can and cannot do. Though many house churches network with other house churches, they still understand themselves to be independent and not dependent on the other churches for oversight.

On the other hand, a cell church may consist of many small home groups (cells), but all of the home groups together comprise the church. No group identifies itself as the church apart from the other groups. These groups are semiautonomous. Each cell makes its own decisions regarding the same afore-mentioned issues, but they do so in light of all the other cells. The pastoral leadership of the church oversees all of the cells; whereas, in a house church network, each house church has its own leadership.

WHAT MAKES THE CHURCHES IN THIS STUDY DIFFERENT FROM OTHER HOUSE CHURCHES?

This book is primarily about house churches that are mis-sional in both their convictions and their practices. Though several books describe house churches, offering several examples of house churches and how to plant house churches, this unique book seeks to address a much neglected area in many writings: the missionary nature of these churches as they presently mani-fest themselves in the United States.

HOW WERE THESE CHURCHES SELECTED?

Locating house churches is not always an easy task. Though websites such as House Church Central (http://www.hccentral.

com/directory) offer a search engine to assist people in locating house churches in their areas, many house churches choose not to register with such databases. There is no central organization that oversees the number of house churches in North America, and since many are nondenominational, denominational headquarters can offer virtually no information on the number of house churches. The churches selected for this study were located through three means. First, Tony Dale with *House2House* magazine (www.house2house.net) assisted greatly with this research. Hearing of my desire to locate and study evangelistic house churches, he willingly emailed several hundred house church leaders with a link to our website where leaders could take our survey. Second, I screened the completed surveys for churches that met the following criteria: (1) they had to baptize at least one person in the last year, and (2) they had to plant at least one church in the past three years. Third, phone interviews were conducted with those church leaders whose churches met the two criteria and were willing to be contacted for a follow-up survey.[24] Of the 255 North American church leaders who participated in our web-based survey, ninety-one churches met both research criteria. Out of these ninety-one churches represented, we contacted thirty-three leaders to participate in our study.

CONCLUSION

As I write these words, I cannot help but think of the first European explorers who landed on the shores of North America. For some, they thought they had discovered new territory, but, in reality, the "new land" was not new at all. People had been living there for many years. Sometimes new discoveries are only new in the eyes of the beholder.

For some of you, I understand that this book is a venture into foreign territory. Though you have heard of this strange new land called "house churches," you have never been there for yourself. Others you have known traveled to this new world and returned to tell you stories about it. I thank you for taking time to enter into this old, yet, "new land." I invite you now to come along prayerfully with our research team into an area of North American church life where few have entered. A warning is necessary: At times the journey will be challenging, convicting, irritating, upsetting, encouraging, edifying, and unusual. This is part of the process of exploring a new domain. My hope is that the trip will be a blessing to you. Above all else, the prayer of our team has been that the Lord would be glorified through our research and this writing.

1

What Is the C/church Anyway?

And on this rock I will build My church, and the forces of Hades will not overpower it.

—Jesus[1]

There is an old story about several blind men standing around an elephant, and each was called on to describe the creature, which none of them had ever encountered before. From their different vantage points, each one could touch and feel a different part of the animal. Feeling the side of the elephant, the first man described the elephant as a wall. The second, grabbing the tusk, exclaimed, "This beast is like a spear!" The third, touching the trunk, noted that the animal was obviously similar to a snake. The fourth man, holding on to the tail, believed that the beast was like a rope. The moral of the story is that, in some sense, each man was correct, but each was also partially wrong.

In North America there are many differing ideas about the Church and the church. In this first chapter we will spend some time examining what the Bible has to say about ecclesiology, the doctrine of the C/church. Concluding this chapter, I will address some of the characteristics of house churches.

The most critical issue facing the expansion of the North American Church today is a theological issue. More specifically, it is an ecclesiological issue. The way we respond to the question, "What is a church?" affects the entire missionary strategy. To use an automobile metaphor, if a missionary team believes that church should look like a Hummer, then everything that team does will revolve around the planting of a church that looks like a Hummer, not a Cadillac, a Ford truck, or a Lamborghini. How we answer this question will impact organization, leadership development, evangelism, worship, and ministries. So, if this question is vitally important, we must begin by asking ourselves, How do we know what we know about the C/church?

SOURCE OF AUTHORITY

People use at least three sources of authority to understand the doctrine of the C/church. First, there is personal subjectivity. Here the source of authority is the human being. I determine what the C/church is. My desire for the C/church is the source of authority and guides me to know what is best. For example, if I do not like the notion of church leaders because they are always causing problems, then I will discard the notion of pastors from my understanding of the church. If I believe that evangelism is outdated and makes me feel uncomfortable, then I will not even consider it for our local congregation.

The problem with this source of authority is that it is too subjective. There is no constant standard by which we can measure truth. What you may believe about C/church could be diametrically opposed to what I may believe; therefore, who is correct and who is incorrect? According to popular philosophies today, we are both correct. Of course, this inconsistency is ludicrous. I find it amazingly foolish that when addressing spiritual issues, we desire relativism; but in other areas of life, we vehemently oppose such subjectivity. For example, if I decided that, in reality, the meaning behind all red stop lights was subjectively determined, and therefore, for me red really meant "go," few relativists would want to approach a traffic intersection if they knew that I was in the oncoming lane. Personal subjectivity is not a healthy source of authority in determining an answer to the question, What is the C/church?

A second yet closely related source of authority in determining church doctrine is that of history, or tradition. Cicero has been attributed as saying, "History is the witness that testifies to the passing of time; it illumines reality, vitalizes memory, provides guidance in daily life and brings us tidings of antiquity."[2] Though Cicero was correct that we could learn much from history, history does not guarantee right belief or practice. Just because Christians have always done church a certain way, or because centuries of cherished tradition form our understanding of church, does not mean that we have a clear and truthful answer to the question, What is the C/church? Just because a community of individuals congregate together and decide what they, as a whole, believe is the best answer to our question does not mean that they are correct. History is filled with numerous groups that became cults and led many astray in the name of Christ with their traditional answers. It is healthy, however, to study Church history and tradition. Such study can assist us in understanding how other brothers and sisters throughout the ages understood the C/church, but history and tradition are not our ultimate source of authority.

The third source of authority, which should be our ultimate source of truth regarding the C/church, is the revelation of God to us through the Bible. Though some have wrongly questioned the authority and reliability of the Scriptures, we must remember that the Scriptures can be trusted and are the only objective source of definitive truth that most accurately answers the question, What is the C/church?

I am amazed at those who claim to be followers of Jesus but deny the authority of His revelation to His Church. For some strange reason, many have no problem believing that God created the heavens and the earth and had the power to raise Jesus from the dead but refuse to believe that this same God was powerful enough to keep the Scriptures pure, maintaining their authority and reliability. We must remember that the same God who accomplished these miracles is the same God who spoke to us through the Scriptures, informing us that "all Scripture is inspired by God and is profitable for teaching, for rebuking, for correcting, for training in righteousness" (2 Timothy 3:16).

Some even doubt that we, being finite creatures, can know any definite truth about an infinite God. This assumption is correct provided the infinite God remains silent and chooses *not* to reveal Himself to His creation. But God is not silent and has chosen to reveal Himself to us through a language we can understand. The writer of Hebrews noted, "Long ago God spoke to the fathers by the prophets at different times and in different ways. In these last days, He has spoken to us by His Son, whom He has appointed heir of all things and through whom He made the universe. He is the radiance of His glory, the exact expression of His nature, and He sustains all things by His powerful word" (Hebrews 1:1–3). Since this God has spoken to us and His words about His Church are reliable, truthful, and authoritative, we must return to the Scriptures to find the answer to the question, What is the C/church?

Before continuing, a word of caution is necessary. When we return to the Scriptures seeking an answer to our question, we may find that some of what we have truly believed is "necessary" for the church to exist comes from personal desires (subjectivity) and history and tradition. These so-called necessities may not necessarily be an evil unto themselves, but when applied to a local church, they may hinder healthy discipleship and thus the rapid spreading of the gospel. These "necessities" may very well be cultural preferences and not biblical requirements. If we discover such components, we must not allow them to have an authority equal to biblical authority, and we must question if indeed these cultural expressions hinder us from a more excellent way of existing as the Church in our Jerusalem, Judea, Samaria, and throughout the world.

EKKLESIA IN THE NEW TESTAMENT

The New Testament, written in Greek, used the word *ekklesia* to describe "C/church." Ekklesia is a compound word consisting of *ek*, meaning "out of," and *klesis*, "a calling." Used one hundred and fourteen times, ekklesia is sometimes translated as "assembly" (three times), "church" (seventy-four times), "churches" (thirty-five times), and "congregation" (two times).[3]

Therefore, whatever the C/church is, it consists of a group of people who have received a calling out of something for a particular purpose.

The uses of ekklesia help increase our understanding of church. For example, in Acts 19:39, 41, the word is used to describe an assembly of people who most definitely were not followers of Jesus. The city of Ephesus was in an uproar because of the power of the gospel. Fearing that the goddess Artemis would be despised, a mob of people rushed into the amphitheater desiring to defend their goddess. Our understanding of ekklesia, therefore, includes the notion of an assembly of people. Another use of this word is found in Stephen's address in Acts 7:38 where ekklesia refers to the assembly of the Israelites in the desert.

Sometimes the word is used to describe the company of believers throughout the ages. For example, in Matthew 16:18, Jesus spoke of building His Church, referring to His present and future followers from every tribe, language, and nation. Paul wrote in Ephesians, "And He put everything under His feet and appointed Him as head over everything for the church, which is His body, the fullness of the One who fills all things in every way" (Ephesians 1:22–23). These two examples show that there is a universal understanding of what exactly constitutes the Church, which differs from a local expression of the Church. In other words, I do not know all the believers who presently live in Africa, but they are my brothers and sisters in Christ. We are part of the body of Christ, the Church, though we may not serve the Lord as a part of the same church.

Many singular forms of the word ekklesia describe this local expression of the universal followers of Christ. For example, in Matthew 18:17 Jesus described how believers should act when one sins against another. If after personal confrontation and the use of two or three witnesses the erring brother remains unrepentant, then the matter should be told to the church. Obviously, Jesus had in mind a local assembly of believers, not the universal Church of all believers. In Acts 20:28 Paul reminded the Ephesian elders that they were shepherds of the church of God, again a local expression. In 1 Corinthians 1:2 and 1 Thessalonians 1:1, Paul addressed the local churches in Corinth and Thessalonica. Again, the word for church describes local expressions in specific places at specific times.

In the New Testament the plural uses of ekklesia refers to local expressions of churches within a geographical region. Describing Paul's travels, Luke wrote, "He traveled through Syria and Cilicia, strengthening the churches" (Acts 15:41). Later, describing the missionary work of Paul and Timothy, he recorded, "As they traveled through the towns, they delivered to them the decisions reached by the apostles and elders at Jerusalem Add: "for them to observe.". So the churches were strengthened in the faith and were increased in number daily" (Acts 16:4–5). Concluding his first letter to the Corinthian church, Paul told the believers, "The churches of the Asian province greet you" (1 Corinthians 16:19). It is clear that in these uses, the apostle had local congregations in mind.

CHURCH: A PERSON, PLACE, OR THING?

Though many believe that in 2 Hezekiah 3:16 we read, "The church is a building with red carpet, a pulpit, at least five rows of pews, and must have a leaky roof," the truth of the matter is that there is no single biblical passage that answers in explicit detail, What is C/church?[4] The Merriam-Webster Online Dictionary defines "church as follows:

- a building for public and especially Christian worship
- the clergy or officialdom of a religious body
- a body or organization of religious believers
- a public divine worship
- the clerical profession[5]

It is evident in these definitions that a church can be a people, a place, and/or a practice. These are radically different concepts, and most in the list are biblically problematic. Here we have a definition that says churches can exist simultaneously as living beings, inanimate objects such as a building, and an event in time.

As a professor at the Southern Baptist Theological Seminary in Louisville, Kentucky, I teach courses in evangelism and church planting. At the beginning of one of my church planting courses, I sometimes lead the class in a "let's imagine" activity. The activity begins when I tell the class that their assignment is to be roving reporters on the streets of Louisville, seeking to answer to the question, What is C/church? They are to venture out into the streets, restaurants, and neighborhoods, recording the responses of the people willing to respond. After spending the day combing the city, they are to return to class and write their responses on the board. In all likelihood, we would have numerous answers, some better than others, but much repetition.

It is at this point in this imaginary reporting experience that I ask the class to give me some of the most common answers. Every time I do this exercise, the following answers are suggested: a group of people, a building, a service you attend on Sundays. After receiving these answers, we begin the second part of the exercise by imagining that they are interviewing people actually entering sanctuaries on Sunday morning. The students are to ask them the same question, What is C/church? and record their responses. At this point, we list on the board what we believe would be the most common responses. The following usually are listed:

- A building
- A group of Christians
- A place you go to worship the Lord
- A worship service (as in, What time is church?)
- Something you do (as in, We had church today.)

After reflecting, the students usually confess that they believe that most of the answers of the unbelievers and believers would be the same. Though our exercise is imaginary, I completely agree with their conclusion: Both those in the kingdom of light and those in the kingdom of darkness understand the C/church to be an animate object, an inanimate object, and an event in time.

In the third step of this exercise I ask the class, How biblical are the responses of many Christians in their understanding of C/church? As we begin to study the Scriptures, we immediately realize that the C/church is *never* a physical structure, a place to go, an event such as "Church is at 11:00 AM," or something you do. The fourth and most poignant step in our exercise is when I ask these students, How many times do you use these nonbiblical descriptors with your congregations while expecting them to have a biblical understanding of the C/church? After this question, there is usually much silence in the room, because we have all used such descriptions.

CITIZENS WITH A KINGDOM ETHIC

So then how do we know what the C/church is from the Scriptures if no concise definition exists? Rather than defining

C/church by what it is not, we need to see what C/church is according to the Scriptures. We can observe Jesus and the apostolic Church in their relationships with one another and with their world. When attempting to understand the nature and functions of the C/church, however, many too quickly turn to Acts and the writings of Paul. Granted, more detailed information regarding the C/church can be located in these two sections of the New Testament; however, we must remember that the apostolic Church was following many of the prescriptions and examples originally established by our Lord. To understand the C/church in the New Testament, we must return to the Gospels.[6]

The Gospels are a genre of literature that address the good news of Jesus. They are not biographies, though they contain biographical material. They are not solely for historic knowledge, though they are historical writings. They are not how-to manuals for witnessing, prosperity, leadership, and a great family life, though we can learn from the principles and examples they contain. The gospels were written so people may believe with certainty that Jesus is the Christ (Luke 1:1–4; John 20:31).

In all of the Gospels, the word ekklesia is only used three times (Matthew 16:18; 18:17). The first time it is mentioned is in the passage of Peter's confession of Jesus as the Christ. The second passage contains Jesus' teaching regarding an erring brother or sister and how the church should respond appropriately. What is clear from the Gospels is that Jesus came to establish a new community, and this community continues to be part of fulfilling the promise to crush the Serpent's head (Genesis 3:15) as well as addressing the promises of the Abrahamic covenant (Genesis 12:1–3). For the apostolic Church, Jesus was the Messiah, and the establishment of this new community called the Church was part of God's plan leading to a new heaven and a new earth (Revelation 21:1).

This new community had a King, but He was unlike any earthly geopolitical ruler. This new community consisted of citizens, but they were unlike the Roman city-state citizens. The citizens of this new community were part of a divine kingdom and lived according to the kingdom ethic that involved 1) love for the King, 2) love for others in the kingdom, and 3) love for those outside the kingdom.

LOVE FOR THE KING

Admittance into this community, and thus the kingdom of God, was not obtainable by birthright (John 3:3) or by keeping part of the King's commandments (Matthew 19:17–22) or by good religious activity (Luke 18:10–14). Admittance into this new community, and thus the expansion of this community, was based on a confession of faith in Jesus as Messiah (Matthew 16:16), love for the Lord (Matthew 22:37), and obedience to all that He commanded (Matthew 28:20). Membership in this community was not based on ostentatious pious acts, but rather an internal, supernatural change of heart (Matthew 23:13–33) and faith like a child (Matthew 18:3). In other words, the Church, universal and local, *must* have a regenerate membership or the New Testament understanding of Church must be discarded. Only upon repentance and faith in Christ does someone become a citizen of the kingdom and thus a member of the Church.

LOVE FOR KINGDOM CITIZENS

A second element in the kingdom ethic is love for others within this new community. So intimate is this love that it is likened to a familial relationship (Matthew 12:46–50; 23:8). Just as in any healthy family, each member serves the other; likewise, these new communities of kingdom citizens are servants to one another. Even the greatest does not escape this paradigm in theory or in practice (Matthew 23:11; John 13:3–15). The citizens of this community are great only when they are the least of all (Mark 9:33–37). Despite the fact that the members of this community are to serve one another, their love is not a passive love. This great love is a bold love that would rather compassionately confront others' sinful lifestyles than simply allow them to continue on the road to destruction and thus bring harm to the entire community (Matthew 18:15–20).

Love for Non-kingdom Citizens

The third component of the kingdom ethic involves love for neighbors. When Jesus was asked about the greatest commandment, He quickly attached love for neighbors to love for the Lord (Matthew 22:36–40). Love for those outside of the community reaches beyond mere sympathy through compassionate actions (Luke 10:29–37). This includes loving our enemies (Matthew 5:44), ministering to those in need, and preaching the message of the kingdom (Mark 1).

Venturing outside of the gospels, we quickly recognize that the apostolic Church continued to live according to the kingdom ethic in relation to God, each other, and the world. Though numerous passages could be listed, the Acts 2:41–47 summary is an excellent example of the Church praising God (v. 47), existing in community with one another (vv. 42, 44–46), finding favor with outsiders, and increasing in numbers as they proclaimed the gospel (v. 47).

Biblical Metaphors

Aside from the examples above, the Scriptures provide us with many metaphors whereby we can gain an understanding of C/church. A metaphor is a phrase that denotes a similarity between two things or concepts. As with the use of all metaphors, the similarity can be carried only so far before it breaks down. For example, if I told my wife that she is a rose, I would naturally be referring to her beauty. Of course, the metaphor loses its meaning when I begin to press it too far, looking for similarities between my wife and the petals of the blossom, the fragrance, the stem, and the need for roses to grow in healthy soil.

On the other hand, sometimes metaphors can be confusing with hidden similarities. How did you know that I was speaking of my wife's beauty when I said she is a rose? I could have been claiming that she is deceptive and hurtful: Though she is beautiful at first glance, like a rose, she will harm you by her subtle thorns![7] The only way to determine the meaning behind the metaphor is to examine the context in which it is used. In our attempt to understand the C/church, we must examine the biblical metaphors in context.

Though these metaphors describe the Church, the only way they can be applied to our Christian faith is through our participation in the church. The Scriptures reveal that the local expression of the body of Christ is where we learn practically to be a family, a fellowship, and a body. Apart from the church, we cannot truly understand the Church.

Family

First, the C/church is described as family. Jesus was once told that His mother and brothers were looking for Him.

Using the opportunity as a teaching moment, He spoke of the relationship among those who are part of the kingdom: "'Who is My mother and who are My brothers?' And stretching out His hand toward His disciples, He said, 'Here are My mother and My brothers! For whoever does the will of My Father in heaven, that person is My brother and sister and mother'" (Matthew 12:46–50). In his letter to the Romans, Paul wrote, "Show family affection to one another with brotherly love. Outdo one another in showing honor" (Romans 12:10). The obvious meaning behind this metaphor is that the bonds holding together the citizens of the kingdom are as strong, if not stronger, than the bond of blood. Just as an earthly family loves, honors, protects, encourages, and cares for one another, the church must do likewise.

Body

Another common metaphor found in the Scriptures is that the C/church is a body, specifically the body of Christ. In Romans and 1 Corinthians Paul spent a significant amount of time painting this picture of the C/church as a body: "Now as we have many parts in one body, and all the parts do not have the same function, in the same way we who are many are one body in Christ and individually members of one another" (Romans 12:4–5). It is clear that just as a human body has different parts and functions, likewise, there are different roles and gifts found within the Church and expressed in the church. Just as the parts of a human body must work in harmony for proper health and function, so there should be unity in the body of Christ (1 Corinthians 12:25).

PRIESTHOOD

Peter wrote that, as followers of Christ, we are a "holy" and "royal priesthood" (1 Peter 2:5, 9). What was the purpose of a priest? In the Old Testament, they represented God before people and they represented the people before God. Peter noted that, as priests, we are "to offer spiritual sacrifices acceptable to God through Jesus Christ" (1 Peter 2:5). Peter continued by citing several Old Testament passages and noting that, as citizens of the kingdom, we "are a chosen race, a royal priesthood, a holy nation, a people for His possession" (1 Peter 2:9). He continued to show why we are given such a lofty connection to the priesthood: "So that you may proclaim the praises of the One who called you out of darkness into His marvelous light" (1 Peter 2:9).

FELLOWSHIP

The C/church is also described as having a common bond or unity with one another that is possible only through a relationship with the King. Many times this bond is referred to as a fellowship or community. John reminds us that we have this fellowship with one another (1 John 1:7). Peter tells us that we should love the brotherhood (1 Peter 2:17). Immediately following Pentecost, the new church was devoted to fellowship (Acts 2:42). This unity is best observed in Acts 4:32–35. Here the love of the brothers and sisters toward one another is clearly displayed.

> Now the multitude of those who believed were of one heart and soul, and no one said that any of his possessions was his own, but instead they held every-

thing in common. And with great power the apostles were giving testimony to the resurrection of the Lord Jesus, and great grace was on all of them. For there was not a needy person among them, because all those who owned lands or houses sold them, brought the proceeds of the things that were sold, and laid them at the apostles' feet. This was then distributed to each person as anyone had a need.

The church had such concern for one another that they were willing to give up their possessions and rights to those goods for the sake of others. This is not an example of Christian communism whereby no one had any personal possessions or control over those possessions. The example of Ananias and Sapphira clearly shows that the fellowship of the body was not some mindless groupthink or practice found in a commune in Jerusalem. After Ananias lied to the Holy Spirit regarding the sale of some land, Peter reminded him, "Wasn't it yours while you possessed it? And after it was sold, wasn't it at your disposal? Why is it that you planned this thing in your heart? You have not lied to men but to God!" (Acts 5:4). The point made is that Ananias had the complete freedom to do with his possessions as he desired, but he chose deception.

The true fellowship is a unity of believers who are willing to make great sacrifices to assist a brother or sister in need. Though there is a commonality to care for all, the widows and orphans are singled out as needing special attention (Acts 6:1; James 1:27; 1 Timothy 5:9). The fellowship of the saints includes carrying one another's burdens (Galatians 6:2) and a relationship whereby it is common and acceptable to confess sins to one another (James 5:16). It is by our love for one another that all people will know that we are the Lord's disciples (John 13:35).

SANCTUARY OR TEMPLE

One of the metaphors used to describe the C/church is that of a sanctuary or temple. In his first letter to the Corinthians, Paul asked, "Don't you know that you are God's sanctuary and that the Spirit of God lives in you?" (1 Corinthians 3:16). This metaphor reveals the powerful truth originally stated by Solomon and later echoed by Stephen that the sovereign God does not dwell in a building made by human hands (1 Kings 8:27; Acts 7:48–49). The gravity of this metaphor by Paul is that the Lord of the universe does not desire to reside in a beautiful, ornate, costly temple, rather He willingly resides in jars of clay (2 Corinthians 4:7). According to Paul, God's sanctuary is holy and, therefore, His followers are holy (1 Corinthians 3:17).

BUILDING

Another metaphor used by Paul and closely connected to the aforementioned one is the Church as a building (Ephesians 2:21). Of course, Paul's application of this metaphor is not that the Church is to become a literal building. As already stated, no reference in the entire Bible refers to the Church, universal or local as a physical building. So what is the context of this metaphor, and how does it affect our understanding of the C/church? In Ephesians 2:19–20 Paul reminded his readers that they are members of God's household, built on the foundation laid by the apostles and prophets. Jesus Himself is the chief cornerstone. In verse 21 Paul added, "The whole building is being fitted together in Him and is growing into a holy sanctuary in the Lord, in whom you also are being built together for God's dwelling in the Spirit" (Ephesians 2:21–22). Echoing Old Testament images, the apostle was probably remembering that both the tabernacle and later the temple in Jerusalem were considered holy places and had to be treated accordingly. Paul was emphasizing the holiness of the Church by reminding His readers that God's standards for his people supersede any other earthly place. Believers become more like Christ as they continue in the sanctification process.

BRIDE

Another common metaphor used to describe the Church is a bride. In Ephesians Paul addressed the relationship between husbands and wives and made a unique comparison of the familial relationship to that of Christ and His Church. Here Paul noted that just as Christ is the head of the Church, the husband is the head of the wife; just as the Church submits to Christ, wives are to submit to their husbands (Ephesians 5:22–24). When Paul told husbands to love their wives, he specifically stated that they are to love them as Christ loved the Church, for Her best, even unto His death (v. 25). Near the end of Revelation, John also wrote of his observations of the bride (Revelation 21:2, 9). This metaphor of the Church conveys something pure and submissive to Christ.

BRANCHES

Jesus used several metaphors to paint a picture of the Church. For example, the Church is also understood as branches connected to Jesus the Vine (John 15:1–8). According to this metaphor, the followers of Jesus must remain attached to Him for survival. Apart from the vine, the branches cannot bear any fruit and are good for nothing.

SHEEP

Jesus also noted that the Church is like sheep (John 10:1–18). Jesus, our Good Shepherd (John 10:14), is one who cares for His sheep. This metaphor clearly reminds us that the C/church is dependent on the Shepherd for protection, leadership, and provision.

SALT AND LIGHT

In the Sermon on the Mount (Matthew 5–7), Jesus referred to His followers as salt and light (Matthew 5:13–17). As salt, the church serves as a seasoning or a preservative, making an impact on societies and cultures for the kingdom. As light, the church sets forth an example of what citizenship in the kingdom looks like. The church reveals the practical outplaying of a kingdom ethic in a dark world. As light, the church lives life in such a manner that others may become worshipers of our Father (Matthew 5:16).

INSTITUTIONAL OR ORGANIC IN NATURE

A comparison of the ways in which many people understand "C/church" and the biblical examples and metaphors used clearly reveals a significant distinction. For the most part, the church today is defined and understood in institutional and compartmentalized concepts.[8] For example, the church in theory and in practice becomes a building, a service, a place, or an event. Missions becomes something we do on the other side of the world or at a homeless shelter. Evangelism is understood as a weeknight visitation program. Worship takes place only a couple hours a week. Discipleship becomes a program. Church membership is diluted to attending worship services and giving financially.

Closely attached to this belief is the notion that ministry becomes a specialization whereby only the professionals can truly understand the Scriptures, minister to the needy, and preach the gospel throughout the world. Another problem coupled with institutionalization is a radical pragmatism, the belief that whatever works (for example, attracts large numbers) is obviously of God. Practically speaking, pragmatism usually forces churches to define success in marketing concepts. Healthy churches are usually labeled as those with the largest numbers in attendance (or baptisms) and the largest financial contributions.

Compartmentalization, or individualization, is a natural bedfellow of institutionalization. The secular separation between the public and private lives of individuals is illustrated by the following theologies of many church members today: "I become a 'part' of the church on Sunday but am free to live my life as I desire throughout the rest of the week," or "What I do in my life is between me and God and no one else," or "I will remain a member of this congregation as long as my family and I get our needs met; if something better comes along, we can always join elsewhere." As noted above, this unhealthy understanding of membership in the body of Christ is completely foreign to the Scriptures. Though it may be popular in Western civilization, the Scriptures clearly show the interdependence of the community. In fact, Paul admonished the Corinthians to judge one of their members because his sexual immorality was harming the church (1 Corinthians 5).

On the other hand, the Scriptures advocate that the Church, particularly the church, is primarily understood in relation to the kingdom of God through organic metaphors emphasizing

1) the relationship of believers to God, 2) the relationship of believers to one another, and 3) the relationship of believers to unbelievers. The church is primarily to be understood in simple relational terms. The definition, function, and vitality of the church does not come from money, sophisticated organization and bureaucracy, numbers, or even a great preacher, but rather from the citizens of the kingdom, indwelled and empowered by God Himself, living according to a kingdom ethic that clearly establishes their relationship with God, each other, and the world.

WHAT IS A HOUSE CHURCH?

Westerners love labels. Partially coming from our scientific minds (as well as our passion for consumerism) is the necessity to identify and label the unfamiliar. This is clearly observed in both the secular and the sacred realm. For example, in an attempt to understand a church, we ask the members, "What type of church is it?" Their responses prove that they understand our question: "Oh, I'm a part of a contemporary church," or "We go to a cell church (or purpose-driven, or seeker-driven)." Some clearly articulate, "My church is a postmodern church," or "We're very traditional," or even "We are a house church."

These labels have been recent developments that assist us in getting a better understanding of congregations. However, my concern is that in a time when consumerism is rampant, we quickly identify churches according to their structure and organization rather than by what they believe and practice, so we can determine if we want to attend that church. Clearly, within the New Testament labels were not an issue, but rather right beliefs and actions were the definitive issues.

Despite my concerns over labels, I am writing a book about churches identified with the label *house*. Since missiology is the science of missions, sometimes we have to create labels in order to identify that which we are studying, even if that label is limiting and not always accurate. It is difficult to speak about what a house church is because not all house churches meet in houses, even though they bear the label *house*.

For example, the House2House website states that house churches go by different names, "house church, simple church, open church, organic church," quickly noting that "these groups can gather anywhere—homes, workplaces, coffee shops, anywhere that people naturally gather!"[9] This was true in our study. All of the respondents clearly understood themselves to be part of house churches, though they may not always gather in houses. Some of the churches periodically gathered in rented facilities.

Though I prefer not to describe the basic essence of most house churches by what they are *not*, sometimes it is necessary to describe the unfamiliar in light of what is familiar. Despite this necessity, I prefer to describe house churches in a "more than, less than" spectrum, rather than the use of "anti-" language, which sounds as if all these churches have a separatist attitude toward other expressions of the body of Christ.

More Organic, Less Institutional

The first and most obvious descriptor of house churches is that they tend to understand themselves in terms of the biblical metaphors mentioned above and less in institutionalized concepts. Individuals who are part of house churches, rarely refer to the local church as a building, place, time, service, event, or activity. Almost always the church is understood as the people, and the language used in house church circles reflects this belief.

Nate Krupp offers an accurate description of what has been oc-curring throughout North America:

> They long for Him to be the Head of His Church. They are gathering in their homes for simple times of worship, sharing their lives with each other, studying the Bible together, praying for one another, having the Lord's Supper together—being a family, rather than an organization. They have an understanding that everyone can minister (1 Corinthians 14:26). Some groups meet in the same home every week, while others move to another home every week or once a month. Some groups are incorporating, while others are being led to have no official connection with the government. Some groups have given themselves a name, while others desire to have no name but His. The leadership styles vary, but most groups have an understanding of getting away from the clergy-laity practice, and look to several to give limited, shared, elder leadership. The groups vary as to their understanding of the role of women. They meet the needs of children in various ways, but generally agree that the training of children in the ways of God is a responsibility of the parents not the Sunday School, junior church, or kids clubs.[10]

MORE SIMPLE, LESS STRUCTURE

House churches constantly guard against rigidity and too much structure and organization. They fear that institutionaliza-tion will begin to take precedence over genuine relationships, thus distorting the simple expression of the faith. For example, the titles of three books written by Tony and Felicity Dale, Robert Fitts, and Nate Krupp, all house church leaders, exemplify this conviction, respectively: *Simply Church; The Church in the House: A Return to Simplicity*; and *God's Simple Plan for His Church and Your Place in It.*[11]

Many house churches try to avoid programs as a means to fulfill their ministries. Though it is a matter of debate whether or not such programs exist, one thing is certain: the word *program* was rarely used by the participants in this study. Many house churches seem to understand programs to be something negative rather than something positive, fearing a program will become an end unto itself and take the place of relationships.

Though some churches use more formalized training, for the most part leadership development, discipleship training, and evangelism and missions generally occur through mentoring relationships and on-the-job training. Also, church planters recognize that it is much easier to see the multiplication of house churches since they are not bound by rigid structures.[12]

More Participatory Worship, Less Passivity

Whenever house churches gather for corporate worship, there is a high level of participation from the members of the congregation. It is common to hear church members reference 1 Corinthians 14:26: "How is it then, brothers? Whenever you come together, each one has a psalm, a teaching, a revelation, another language, or an interpretation. All things must be done for edification." According to some house church leaders, the principle found here is that everyone has an active role in the corporate gathering of the church. Rusty Entrekin commented,

There is a very important word in 14:26 that is usually ignored. It is the word "everyone." The text does not say, "When you come together, the minister of music has a song, and the pastor has a word of instruction." Instead, it tells us that "everyone" comes with the potential to contribute something. Since this is the case, shouldn't we give everyone the opportunity to do so? This verse makes it startlingly clear that God does not intend for pastors to be the only people who are allowed to bring a word of instruction during church, or ministers of music the only ones who introduce songs to sing![13]

More Community, Less Acquaintances

House church members emphasize genuine community, and surface-level friendships are unusual. House churches see the value of genuine fellowship and make nurturing relationships a normal part of church membership. Along with this emphasis on community is an emphasis on transparency and accountability that encourages bearing one another's burdens, the confession of sin, and church discipline. It is common to hear people reference Hebrews 10:24–25 when discussing community: "And let us be concerned about one another in order to promote love and good works, not staying away from our meetings, as some habitually do, but encouraging each other, and all the more as you see the day drawing near."

More ministers, Less Ministers

Believing that the Reformation prohibited a healthy unleashing of the laity, the House Church Movement in North

America has worked hard to elevate the responsibilities of church members and what it means for them to be involved in ministry. Unfortunately, some house churches have reacted negatively to professional clergy, even to the degree that some have jettisoned the office of the pastor/elder. For example,

> Although all house churches are different, and they decide individually how they want to do things, in general there are no "pastors." At least there doesn't need to be. We believe that the Holy Spirit can use any believer to teach or encourage the group. In a house church, everyone is expected to participate and be looking for ways to use the gifts the Holy Spirit provides (see 1 Corinthians 14:26).
>
> Certainly there is usually a facilitator of the group (although it doesn't need to be the same person that facilitates from meeting to meeting). We believe that even a new believer could start a church in their home without feeling like they need a trained professional to come and lead it, or needing money to support such a person. We find that the lack of a specified pastor encourages every person in the group to look for answers by searching the Scriptures and looking to the Holy Spirit, rather than depending on the pastor to interpret.[14]

Rather than hoping church members will eventually find their place of service, most house churches promote an atmosphere that every member is a minister with Christ as the Head, and all are required to use their gifts and serve the body. While I am in complete support of more ministers of the gospel and greatly appreciate the work to remove the clergy/laity dichotomy,

I am troubled by the discarding of pastors/elders in some of the churches. Thankfully, not all house churches have followed this troubling path. I will address the matter of pastoral leadership in a later chapter.

CONCLUSION

House churches are not new; in fact, they have been around for two thousand years. And though they have existed for some time in North America, only recently has this expression of the body of Christ started to gain the interest of those outside of house churches. The simplicity, community, and high level of participation that is required in this expression of church is appealing to many. Though the churches in our study hold much in common with other house churches, the unique characteristic for our study was the fact they were indeed making disciples and planting churches.

It is now time to meet the churches that made it into our study.

2

Meet the
Missional House Churches

*The meeting of two personalities is like the
contact of two chemical substances:
if there is any reaction, both are transformed.*

—CARL JUNG, SWISS PSYCHOLOGIST, 1875–1961

*I told my psychiatrist that everyone hates me.
He said I was being ridiculous—
everyone hasn't met me yet.*

—RODNEY DANGERFIELD, COMEDIAN, 1921–2004

First impressions? They are most definitely important.
Whether you are meeting a great leader, going to a job interview,

or meeting the parents of your spouse-to-be, introductions are critical. It is true that we never get to make a second first impression. This chapter offers a first impression of the churches that made it into this study. This chapter is divided into four primary sections. The first addresses the demographical matters related to the churches. The second section is a brief discussion of the theological beliefs of the churches. The third section introduces you to the leaders who participated in this study. Finally, this chapter concludes by addressing the structure and organization of many house churches.

DEMOGRAPHICS

In this study, the team examined matters related to the locations, ethnic make-ups, ages, generational consistencies, and sizes of the churches. Though it cannot be stated with certainty regarding all house churches, it must be noted that the churches in this study represented a great amount of demographic diversity.

LOCATIONS

Of the thirty-three churches that made it into this study, seventeen states were represented. Because of the difficulty locating churches for our study, we were unable to take representative samples from the various regions of North America (see appendix 1). Despite this situation, we did have participants from the East, Northeast, Southeast, Midwest, Southwest, Northwest, West, and Pacific regions. Unfortunately, no Canadian churches were represented in our findings.

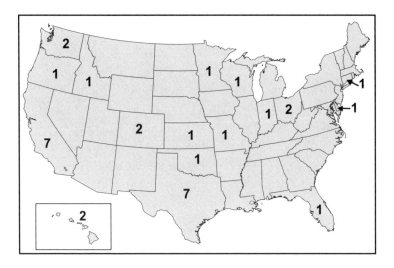

Not Limited by Population Density

As I have traveled this continent and spoken with many church and denominational leaders and read numerous publications regarding house churches, time and again I have heard polarized comments such as, "House churches are an urban phenomenon," and "The rural environment is where house churches will work the best because populations are so sparse," or one of the most popular, "House churches only work in persecuted, preindustrial societies. Just look at China and the developing world." Although we were unable to offer a large representative geographical sample of North America house churches, the missional house churches in our study were located in a variety of population densities.

For example, one church in Minnesota identified itself as meeting in an open country/rural area. On the other hand, a church leader from Long Beach, California, noted that his church met in a large city/downtown or inner city (50,000+

population). A church leader from Broken Arrow, Oklahoma, stated that his congregation was a part of a small city (2,500–9,999 population), while several other leaders noted that their churches met in large city/suburbs (50,000+ population). A church in Post Falls, Idaho, was located in a medium city/suburban area of approximately 18,000 people. Our team interviewed another leader whose congregation gathered in a medium city/downtown (10,000–49,000 population) location, while another church was located in Eagle Creek, Oregon, a town just outside of metropolitan Portland. Additional research is necessary to determine if certain contexts are more conducive for the existence of house churches. We can state, however, that missional house churches cannot be limited to a particular location based on the population, rural, suburban, or urban contexts.

Predominately Caucasian, But Much Ethnic Diversity

During the data-gathering phase of our research, I met periodically with my research team to discuss our findings. This process initially led me to assume that our survey work would probably reveal many congregations were predominately Caucasian. Though this assumption proved correct, the ethnic diversity represented in the churches surprised me. Less than one-third of the leaders surveyed noted that their congregations were 100 percent Caucasian. The majority of the churches were ethnically diverse.[1]

One network leader in Austin noted about a 5 percent Hispanic representation in their churches. A church network in Thousand Oaks, California, had a small representation of African Americans, Latinos, and Hawaiian Asians.

Though the findings are inconclusive, these churches may have statistically greater racial/ethnic representation than most traditional congregations in North America. For example, a house church of twenty people, five of whom are African American and one Hispanic, statistically has 30 percent of its congregants non-Caucasian. A congregation of two hundred people, however, would need fifty African Americans and ten Hispanics to be statistically equivalent. Though this latter situation exists in traditional congregations, it is not common throughout North America.

One congregation in Washington state was estimated to be at least 3 percent African American and 2 percent Asian. A congregation in Houston was 2.5 percent African American and 2.5 percent Hispanic. In Kailkua-Kona, Hawaii, 20 percent of one house church was non-Caucasian. A church leader in Colorado commented that one house church in their network consisted of 50 percent Asians and Hispanics. In Texas, one leader noted that they had a representation of 20 percent Hispanic and 10 percent African American. A congregation in Minnesota consisted of 2 percent Eastern Indians, 1 percent Asian, and 1 percent African American.

In Boyceville, Wisconsin, one-third of one congregation was American Indian. Another church in Columbus, Ohio, consisted of one-quarter African Americans. A church leader in southern California shared with the team that his church consisted of 30 percent Chinese and 30 percent Hispanic, while another nearby leader stated a 35–40 percent Hispanic representation, 2 percent African American, and a small representation of Cambodians as well. It should be noted that this leader stated that at one time, they had seven languages represented.

MOSTLY NEW CHURCHES

Almost 80 percent of the churches in our study had been meeting together for less than ten years. Twenty-one percent of the churches were at least ten years old. Of the thirty-three churches, many were recently planted (under six years of age). Forty-six percent of the churches had been meeting together for one to three years at the time of our study. Thirty percent had been meeting for four to six years. Two churches in the study had been meeting for ten to twelve years, while only one church had been meeting for less than one year. Five churches—in California, Texas, Minnesota, Wisconsin, and Missouri—had been meeting for thirteen or more years.

NOT JUST GROUPS OF GENERATION X

Our team had a difficult time obtaining the percentages of the ages of the people making up fourteen of the churches in our study. We were able to get nineteen of the church leaders to provide us with the desired information. Despite the difficulty, it was clear that these churches were not exclusively for the Baby Buster generation. Of the nineteen, only six leaders (32 percent) stated that the largest percentage of their churches was nineteen to thirty-five year olds (two of the leaders stated that 100 percent of the people in their churches were nineteen to thirty-five years of age; one leader stated 80 percent were nineteen to thirty-five; another leader stated 90 percent were nineteen to thirty-five).

Though Larry Kreider and others have noted that house

churches are "for a new generation" (nineteen to thirty-five year olds), I greatly fear that many have been quick to stereotype house churches as an expression of church primarily for younger generations.[2] I must confess that I entered into this study assuming there would be little generational differentiation among the churches; I was wrong. It was clear that most of the churches in our study were made up largely of younger people (fifty years or less); however, there was a great diversity among the ages. The response of one church leader in California could have applied to several of the churches in this study. Commenting on the ages in the church, he said, "It is a pretty doggone good spread here from infant to 70s."

The following examples taken from a few of the churches paint the picture of the age distribution that we encountered time and again:

Congregation	Under 18	19–35	36–50	51–65
1	30%	30%	30%	10%
2	30%	15%	55%	0%
3	65%	20%	10%	5%
4	30%	50%	20%	0%
5	20%	40%	30%	10%

TABLE 1
A Sample of Age Distribution

SIZES OF THE CHURCHES

There are differing opinions on the average size of North American churches. Lyle Schaller, in his article "What is Your Definition of Small," commented, "Likewise the evidence suggests the normative size for an American Protestant congregation is somewhere between 25 and 40 at worship."[3] Smallchurch. com stated, "75% of America's churches have an average weekly attendance of 150 or less."[4] In 2001 the Hartford Institute for Religion Research published a comprehensive study of both Christian and non-Christian congregations noting, "Half of congregations have fewer than 100 regularly participating adults."[5] Though not all house churches are small, usually their sizes are much smaller than most traditional North American churches. In fact, the size of these house churches has contributed to some seeing them as less than "real" churches, or not even churches at all.

When asked, "When your individual house church gathers for worship and fellowship, what is usually the size of the church present?" the average range of the churches represented in our study was between fourteen to seventeen people. There was one church in our study that was larger than thirty-four people, and three churches averaged six to nine participants.

THEOLOGICAL BELIEFS

Though we can learn much from tradition and reason, God's revelation to us in the Bible is our sole source of authority. Through God's Word we know and understand Him, grasp our sinfulness, see the forgiveness and life Christ offers, and understand our place in the body of Christ and in mission to the world. What we believe about the teachings of God's Word affects everything we do in the fellowship of the church. Though our study was not to offer a detailed analysis of the theological beliefs of the leaders surveyed, it was extremely important to ask churches' views on the Scriptures, salvation, church member-ship, tithes/offerings, and elders and deacons.

HIGH VIEW OF THE SCRIPTURES

Ninety-seven percent of those who participated in our study clearly showed a great respect for and a conservative theological perspective of the trustworthiness of the Bible. All the leaders, except for one, either agreed or strongly agreed that "the Bible is the Word of God without any error." During our phone interviews, it was not unusual to hear these leaders state, "The Bible says . . ." to support the practices of their churches. One stereotype that presently surrounds the house church expression of the body of Christ is that many such groups are casting the Scriptures aside and following divergent whims, desires, or beliefs. Though this may be true in some situations, the leaders from our study deeply rooted their beliefs and practices in the Bible. They attempted to be biblical in faith and practice.

YOU MUST BE BORN AGAIN!

Given that almost all of these leaders had a very high view of the Scriptures, it was no surprise that they clearly supported an evangelical understanding of salvation. When asked, "Please describe in some detail what your church believes must take place for a person to be born again," leaders' responses contained phrases such as:

- Repentance and faith in Christ
- Romans 10:9–10
- Confess with your mouth; believe in your heart

- Surrender and commitment to Christ
- Repent of a sinful lifestyle; accept Christ as personal Savior and Lord
- Recognition of sin, asking forgiveness, making Him Lord
- Allegiance to Jesus as Lord
- Regeneration by the Holy Spirit; gift of God for saving faith

Through conversations with church leaders of different denominations, I have noticed a growing problem within the North American Church related to evangelism. Today there is a desire to redefine what evangelism is. This change tends to manifest itself with a hesitancy to call people to repentance of their sin nature (Luke 13:3), and it substitutes a verbal proclamation of the gospel with *primarily* living a good life before the unbelieving world. Therefore, I entered into this research fearing that the leaders of these churches would have embraced this popular and false theology of evangelism. Thankfully I was wrong in my assumption.

Though I say more about their methods of evangelism in chapter 3, the churches in this study emphasize evangelism occurring through relationships. The leaders in these churches realize that the preaching of the gospel must include lifestyle witnessing. They expressed no shame regarding the necessity of a person's repentance to God and faith in the Lord Jesus (Acts 20:21). There seemed to be no hesitation for them or their churches in calling people to this level of commitment. Though these churches were significantly involved in developing relationships with unbelievers, they clearly understood that a verbal proclamation of the gospel message was necessary for salvation.

MEMBERSHIP

The New Testament is clear that though there may be unbelievers present in the church's corporate gathering (1 Corinthians 14:24–25), only those who have been born again that are members of that community called the church (1 Corinthians 12:12–14). Membership is not optional at either the universal or local level (1 Corinthians 12).

Though I recognize that George Barna's book *Revolution* is very popular, he has greatly deviated from the biblical teaching regarding our responsibility to the local church. Barna wrote, "Whether you become a Revolutionary immersed in, minimally involved in, or completely disassociated from a local church is irrelevant to me (and, within boundaries, to God). What matters is not whom you associate with (i.e., a local church), but who you are."[6] Fruit-bearing discipleship in a church, however, is a requirement for our obedience. True revolutionaries are members of *both* the universal and the local church.

Some church leaders are discarding a biblical understanding of church membership, including unregenerate individuals as equals in the church community. For example, Eddie Gibbs and Ryan K. Bolger quoted Anna Dodridge saying, "One great thing about this community-type church . . . is that we can involve non-Christians in our community. They can hang out with us, eat with us, and get served by us. That to me is evangelism as it should be. People can belong to the community and really get an idea about our day-to-day lifestyle."[7] It is one thing to practice the ministry of hospitality and welcome the unbeliever, but it is clearly unbiblical to allow both the regenerate and unregenerate to belong in the community known as the church. In the community (that is church), such equality does not exist.

Though our study asked no questions to determine where house church leaders stood on these contemporary trends, it was clear that church membership in their churches has been stripped of much cultural tradition. Though we have no percentages, some house church leaders have discarded the notion of a church roll or membership roster, believing that membership is based more on intimate relationships and gift use. We quickly noticed the difficulty in asking questions about membership requirements. Our survey tool was written with a common understanding of membership in mind, whereby the believer joins a local church and has his or her name added to the church's membership list. When asked, "Are there any requirements/expectations (for example, attending a new members' class, signing a covenant) for being a member of your house church?" thirteen of the leaders (39 percent) noted that their churches did have requirements for membership. On the other hand, twenty leaders (61 percent) had no requirements/expectations for membership. Because of the wording of our survey, I believe more of these latter leaders did indeed have certain requirements/expectations in place. For example, when asked about assimilation (see below), leaders with no membership requirements offered many of the same responses as leaders in churches with requirements/expectations. For the 39 percent, however, follow-up questions were asked about their requirements/expectations. Several responded with "baptism," "membership class," "participation," involvement in "discipling groups," or commitment to "life transformation groups."

I was also concerned about the overall assimilation process found in these churches. Assimilation is a contemporary term describing how churches make certain that recent converts are actively using their gifts in building up the body and bearing much fruit. A simple open-ended question probed for this understanding: "How does your church know when a believer has a sense of belonging and is thus involved in the life and ministry of the church?" We consistently heard responses (both from churches with and those without membership requirements/expectations) for membership that included "participation," "involvement," "attendance," "relationship development," "full engagement in the community of the church," "sharing life together," and "transparency."

Though many of these churches represented probably had no official membership rolls, they did have what seems to be an unwritten guide to official membership and assimilation. This guide was based on life-on-life interaction within the community of believers. To become a member was to become a member of a family in which there were expectations for everyone involved. Obviously, the size of these congregations made accountability very possible. At this level of intimacy, it is much easier to encourage one another and to promote love and good works (Hebrews 10:24–25).

Without a membership roll or covenant, it was not clear how these churches practiced corrective church discipline. Even with house churches, I have found that it is difficult to call people to accountability if the church does not know who is on board. Pastoral care and corporate decision-making become difficult as well. Future research should also take into consideration the weaknesses in our survey tool related to assimilation.

WEEKLY GATHERINGS

Like most churches, the churches in our study gathered weekly for worship and fellowship. Only four of the thirty-three churches (12 percent) had no weekly gathering. All the churches, except one, gathered in houses for worship and fellowship.

Tithes and Offerings

Though most of the churches in our study give the majority of their financial income to missions and ministry efforts (see chapter 4), the churches were fairly divided on the issue of when to collect such gifts. Answers to the question, "Does your individual church regularly collect financial tithes/offerings?" were interesting. Though we did not define "regularly," seventeen of the respondents noted that the churches did regularly collect such monies. On the other hand, fourteen respondents stated that their churches did not collect on a regular basis. Money and house churches are discussed in a later chapter.

Baptisms and Church Planting

When I first began this study, I was interested in understanding more about churches that were *both* baptizing and planting other churches. One of the screening criteria for this study was to determine which churches had recently experienced these two activities. Again, we must be cautious drawing too many conclusions from a study of such chronological brevity. Much more research needs to be done examining missional house churches over a longer period of time. My assumption was that most of the house churches in North America would be newly planted churches themselves, unable to provide several years of data. For this reason, we asked for data only from the past few years.[8]

In North America, 255 house church leaders participated in our initial web-based survey. Of these, 146 churches experienced at least one baptism in the previous year, and 123 planted at least one church within the past three years. Obviously, we praised the Lord for these churches and what they were doing to make disciples. However, on further examination, we determined that 91 churches baptized at least one person in the previous year *and* planted at least one other church within the previous three years.

The average number of baptisms for each of the thirty-three churches in the study was four to six people for the previous year. Seventeen of the thirty-three churches were at least four years old and therefore able to provide additional baptismal data. Each of these seventeen churches also averaged four to six baptisms per year for the past three years.

When asked, "In the past three years, how many churches has your church planted?" (a question that could be answered by all thirty-three churches, regardless of their age) the average number of churches started by each congregation was four to six churches. Twenty-one of the churches (64 percent) each planted between one and three churches, and three churches (9 percent) had each planted ten or more congregations. In chapter 3, I address the issues of evangelism and church growth in missional house churches.

ELDERS AND DEACONS

The survey asked about church leadership at the local level and at the network level for those churches affiliated with a network. Twenty-eight (85 percent) of the leaders surveyed stated that pastors/elders were a part of their individual house church's leadership. However, when asked if deacons were a part of their individual house church's leadership, unfortunately, only thirteen (39 percent) stated in the affirmative. For those churches involved in a network, the majority of the leaders acknowledged that elders oversaw the networks as well as the local churches. I will address the issue of elders and deacons until chapter 3.

When the respondents were asked about the responsibilities of the elders overseeing networks, they gave a variety of responses. Some of the responsibilities included shepherding the churches, maintaining doctrinal purity, teaching, exhorting, correcting, and rebuking. Other elder responsibilities involved facilitating meetings, casting vision, handling finances, evangelism, training leaders, planting churches, and serving as a spiritual father to the churches.

Survey Participants

Having some knowledge of the leaders in house churches greatly assisted us in understanding those churches. The participants clearly identified themselves as leaders in house churches. For the most part, they were highly educated. Our study removed the stereotype that leaders are involved in house churches because they are uneducated and, therefore, are not eligible to serve in more established church settings.

Twenty-five of the thirty-three leaders surveyed (76 percent) had a college degree level of education or higher, with the average level of education consisting of some graduate studies. Our team noted that some of these leaders were alumni of Northwest Graduate School, Fuller Theological Seminary, Southwestern Baptist Theological Seminary, Asbury Theological Seminary, Concordia Seminary, Denver Seminary, Grace Theological Seminary, and Talbot Theological Seminary. Of the leaders surveyed, four had doctoral degrees and two had completed some doctoral studies.

One interesting discovery arose from leaders' confusion when asked, "What are your primary responsibilities as a house church leader?" This confusion was not because they failed to understand their responsibilities, but the problem was with our survey instrument, which assumed that each of these leaders was attached to only one congregation. In reality, many of them ministered to several congregations. Much like modern-day circuit riders, these leaders ministered from church to church. However, many local congregations had their own elders, with our survey participants serving in a more apostolic role.

A word of clarification is necessary at this point. For many, reading the word *apostolic* conjures up thoughts that these leaders see themselves on par with the twelve apostles in the New Testament. Though our survey did not seek to understand their definition of the word *apostolic*, my conversations with many of them did reveal a different definition of the word.

Many of these leaders saw themselves functioning primarily as church planters, teachers, leadership developers, and mentors/coaches for local church pastors/elders. They leaders were overseeing and leading networks of churches, rather than a single congregation. It was in these ways that many understood themselves to be apostolic.

These leaders led primarily out of a *relational* authority granted to them from the churches, rather than a leading from a *positional* authority because they had a certain title. Some leaders spoke of the necessity of setting the example of the way of a disciple by modeling the Christ-like lifestyle before the churches. Others noted the importance of modeling hospitality before the brothers and sisters. Many of these leaders are significantly involved in coaching church leaders, protecting the churches, preaching/teaching, encouraging, and discipling.

STRUCTURE AND ORGANIZATION

I still find children's kaleidoscopes fascinating. By twisting the simple toy, the viewer creates a multitude of colorful patterns. This device uses colored bits of material, mirrors, and light to create images that are highly diverse and unique. The churches in our study were structured and organized in a variety of ways. Like the images seen in a kaleidoscope, we can expect diversity in these expressions of church life.

In fact, if there are common structural threads that connect most house churches, it is the fact that they strive to be very low in structure and organization with a decentralized leadership, and they place a high degree of emphasis on community. In an attempt to better understand these missional house churches, I have identified at least three different ways house churches tend to organize themselves. It should be noted that, in some cases, these types are not mutually exclusive, with some churches falling into more than one category.

ISOLATIONISTS

The first way that some churches organize themselves is through isolation. These churches believe they should have no accountability with other churches—they are an island unto themselves and have no desire to minister with other local expressions of the body of Christ. Though many opponents of house churches tend to stereotype all such churches as isolationists, my hope is that this type of church is the exception rather than the norm. Our study did not reveal any such churches.[9] In fact, we discovered newly planted independent churches that desired to unite with other churches.

NETWORKERS

The networker churches see themselves as independent (autonomous), but they understand the biblical example, importance, and wisdom in networking with other churches. For these congregations, they choose to be *interdependent*, working with other autonomous congregations for missionary work, benevolence, leader training, accountability, and fellowship. Though these congregations are self-governing, self-supporting, self-propagating, self-teaching, and self-expressing, they realize that there is biblical support for interdependence and the ability to accomplish more for the kingdom while working together as opposed to being isolationists. Many of these networks were local; that is, the churches were close geographically. On the other hand, some of the networks were regional, national, and even international in scope.

Twenty-five of the churches in our study (76 percent) were affiliated with a network of house churches. Most of these networks consisted of two to fourteen churches. Thirty-six percent (twelve churches) were affiliated with networks consisting of three to five congregations. Some of the networks had no official name, but many did.

For most churches affiliated with a network, at least one time each year all of the churches gathered as a whole for worship and fellowship. Twenty of the leaders in our study noted that all of the churches within their networks did regularly meet as a network. Only two leaders stated that all the churches in their networks did not gather regularly.[10] When asked how often the network of churches met, two leaders responded, "At least once a week." One noted, "At least twice per month." Eight leaders stated that the churches gathered "at least every three weeks," (the most common answer by our respondents). One leader commented that the network gathers every three months. Two networks gather at least every quarter. One network gathers at least twice per year. Two leaders stated that their networks met at least once a year. Though these networks usually gather in a large house, some networks rent a neutral public area in which to meet.

DENOMINATIONALS

With the penchant for low organization and structure and a decentralized base of authority common among many house churches, it should be of no surprise that most house churches were not affiliated with denominations. Though in our study this situation was clearly the case, there were five churches that identified themselves with four denominations: Disciples of Christ, Church of Christ, Grace Brethren, and the Southern Baptist Convention.

When I asked one leader what his denomination thought of their network of churches, he responded that they were looked on unfavorably by the denomination. He was quick to add that they were considering separating from the denomination because of theological differences. According to him, the denomination believed the house churches were too "conservative," and the house churches refused to agree with the denomination's general belief that Jesus was "someone who was just a good guy."

While serving in my denomination, I have had the privilege

of speaking with numerous leaders over the years. In private and public conversations, I have been impressed at the growing number of denominational and local church leaders who are very supportive of house churches. Though some may find this fact a bit of a surprise, in reality, my denomination has been planting simple expressions of local churches for a long time. Though this strategy has continued for the most part outside of North America, it does occur here as well. In fact, there are state conventions and local associations of churches who are working to plant Southern Baptist churches that are low in structure and highly committed to the Scriptures, missions, interdependence (cooperation), and relationships.

CONCLUSION

The house churches in our study represented a variety of geographic regions across North America. From rural to urban, and from small town to large city, house churches can be found. Our team discovered that though many of the churches in our study are predominately Caucasian, there is a great deal of ethnic diversity represented as well. The majority of these churches are not primarily Generation X churches, and they are led by pastors/elders who subscribe to conservative evangelical views. The participants in our study are highly educated and provide oversight to several churches. None of the churches in our research was isolationist, but rather the majority functioned in networks.

If our study has caused you to ask additional questions about North American house churches, then one of my reasons for writing has been accomplished. I even had additional questions at the completion of this project. House church life needs to be examined and reported. Better survey instruments need to be developed. Additional research is needed to address other questions. For example, what about the roles of women in house churches? Why are some house churches not advocating the role of deacon? Why are some churches refusing to have pastors/elders? What is the life span of newly planted churches? For those churches planted three years ago, how many still exist and function as churches today? What is done to reclaim members of house churches who drop out of the fellowship? Without a membership roll or covenant, how do house churches practice corrective church discipline? For house churches that have affiliated with denominations, what are the requirements to affiliate and to continue in a partnership?

3
_____

Church Growth and Missional House Churches

So the preaching about God flourished, the number of the disciples in Jerusalem multiplied greatly, and a large group of priests became obedient to the faith.

—LUKE[1]

Following a recent survey regarding the spiritual commitment of North American Christians, George Barna noted, "Evangelism is not a priority in most churches, so the fact that most churched adults do not verbally share the gospel in a given year is not deemed problematic. Only one out of every eight churches bothers to evaluate how many of their congregants are sharing their faith in Christ with non-believers."[2] Roger W. Gehring, in his scholarly work *House Church and Mission: The Importance of Household Structures in Early Christianity*, wrote, "Past and present speak a clear message: By no means should the house church model be overlooked today as a viable option for church growth; it is a tried and tested approach."[3]

This chapter is divided into two sections. In the first, I address the concept of church growth, while asking such questions as, "What is church growth?" and "How do churches grow?" The second half of this chapter examines church growth issues as they manifested themselves in the missional house churches in our study.

WHAT IS CHURCH GROWTH?

In 1955 Donald McGavran, a missionary to India, published a book entitled *The Bridges of God*. Though this book would not become popular for several years, it quietly started a revolution in the Church, birthing the modern-day Church Growth Movement that revolved around two simple questions: "Why do churches grow?" and "How do churches grow?" Thom S. Rainer, in *The Book of Church Growth*, stated, "Church growth is that discipline which seeks to understand, through biblical, sociological, historical, and behavioral study, why churches grow or decline. True church growth takes place when 'Great Commission' disciples are added and are evidenced by responsible church membership."[4] Since McGavran was the father of this modern movement, I will briefly examine some of his thoughts on the sources and types of church growth as found in his book *Understanding Church Growth*.[5]

SOURCES OF GROWTH

There are three sources of church growth. The first source is biological growth. As families that make up churches experience the birth of children into their homes, naturally the church family grows as well. Following a birth, another body is present and taking up space. The church's nursery now has one less available crib. As I write these words, my wife and I are expecting our third child. In fact, there are two other ladies in our congregation expecting children. Lord willing, within the year, our church family will grow by at least three people.

The second source of growth is transfer growth, the most common form of growth in the North American Church. Transfer growth occurs when believers from one congregation move, or transfer, their membership to another congregation. When my family and I moved from Indianapolis, Indiana, to Louisville, Kentucky, we were very thankful that there was a church with which we could unite in our new location.

Conversion growth is the third source of church growth. It occurs when someone moves from the kingdom of darkness into the kingdom of light. As people come to faith in Christ, local churches grow.

Though all of these are sources of church growth, *only* conversion growth can be supported as a *biblical* kind of church growth. There is no Scriptural evidence for biological or transfer growth. Biological and transfer growth do not result in kingdom growth and will not directly result in reaching the world for Christ.

When the ladies in our church give birth to their children, though our church family will grow by numbers and will celebrate the arrivals, the kingdom has not grown. Though these children will be born into Christian families, their genealogy does not make them believers and citizens of the kingdom. Just as Jesus told Nicodemus that his heritage was not sufficient to enter into the kingdom and that he had to be born again (John 3:7), likewise, these little ones must come to faith before the kingdom grows.

Though my wife and I moved from fellowship with one church in central Indiana to unite in fellowship with a church in Louisville, the kingdom did not expand. The church in Louisville grew by a couple of members, but the kingdom of darkness was not pushed back—no one came to faith in Christ since we were already believers

The Scriptures are clear: as followers of Jesus go into the entire world, they are to make disciples, baptize, and teach them to obey all that Christ commanded (Matthew 28:19–20). The example that follows in the rest of the New Testament is one that expects this process (evangelizing, baptizing, teaching) to occur within the context of the local expressions of the body of Christ—churches. As this process is played out across the globe, local churches, and thus the entire body of Christ (universal), grow. Our Lord expected conversion growth to be the normative pattern by which the Church grows.

FOUR TYPES OF CHURCH GROWTH

In light of the three sources of growth, there are four types of growth whereby these sources are expressed. Missiologists commonly refer to these types of growth as internal, expansion, extension, and bridging.

INTERNAL GROWTH

Internal growth is commonly referred to as spiritual growth. When the church matures in faith, internal growth occurs. Three people in your church who begin sharing their faith with non-Christians is an example of internal growth. Whenever someone begins to study and apply the Scriptures to his or her life, internal growth occurs. Paul spoke of internal growth when he wrote, "Work out your own salvation with fear and trembling. For it is God who is working in you, enabling you both to will and to act for His good purpose" (Philippians 2:12–13). This form of growth is obviously difficult to quantify but, nevertheless, should always be occurring in the lives of believers until the day of their glorification.

Another understanding of internal growth, one that is probably not relevant to the churches in our study, is that of structural growth. When a church decides to expand its physical structures (seating capacity, parking spaces), a type of internal growth occurs. The construction of buildings falls into this understanding of growth.

EXPANSION GROWTH

When most people hear the words *church growth* they immediately think of expansion growth, also known as numerical growth. As biological, transfer, and conversion growth occur, churches grow by expansion. Even a cursory reading of the book of Acts reveals that the church in Jerusalem grew through conversion growth. Three thousand people were added to the church following Peter's Pentecost sermon (Acts 2:41). As the gospel was preached, "the number of the disciples in Jerusalem multiplied greatly, and a large group of priests became obedient to the faith" (Acts 6:7). Following the deaths of Ananias and

Sapphira, we read, "Believers were added to the Lord in increasing numbers—crowds of both men and women" (Acts 5:14). After Saul's conversion, Luke recorded, "So the church throughout all Judea, Galilee, and Samaria had peace, being built up and walking in the fear of the Lord and in the encouragement of the Holy Spirit, and it increased in numbers" (Acts 9:31).

I was not interested in studying house churches in general but rather wanted to better understand those churches experiencing expansion growth *through* conversions. For some time I had heard people assume that house churches were inwardly focused. "We four and no more!" some would sarcastically say, expressing what they believed to be a common mantra among house churches. I wanted to know, however, who was reaching people and seeing expansion growth.

The overwhelming majority of the churches in North America are not growing. Thom Rainer, president of Lifeway Christian Resources,[6] stated, "The reality is that about 96 percent of the churches in America do not meet the criteria for being effective evangelistic churches."[7] Due to a lack of data, I cannot speak for other denominations; however, I can report my statistics. Southern Baptists are known as one of the most evangelistic and missions-minded denominations on the planet. Though I am proud to be a Southern Baptist and encouraged by our desire to reach others with the gospel, our statistics are not encouraging. Presently, over 80 percent of our churches are not experiencing substantial expansion growth. For example, of the approximately 43,000 churches that comprise the Southern Baptist Convention, at least 13,465 (31.3 percent) experienced no baptisms in 2003.[8] When the churches that baptized only one individual in 2003 are factored into the statistics, the number jumps to 16,723 (38.5 percent).[9]

In the house church research, I intentionally set the standards very low, looking for house churches that had experienced at least one baptism in the year prior to our study. The reason for such a low standard is that thousands of churches (both denominational and non-denominational) in North America do not baptize any person in a given year. In developing our screening paradigms, I assumed that since many churches are not baptizing, then it was likely that many house churches were doing likewise.

Of the 255 churches that participated in our online survey, 146 churches experienced at least one baptism in the previous year. The thirty-three churches that made it into our study (having experienced both baptisms and church planting) had *an average of four to six baptisms per church* in the previous year.

Membership to Baptism Ratio

A common statistic in church growth studies used to measure evangelistic effectiveness is the membership to baptism ratio. This number states the number of people it takes for a particular congregation to baptize one person in a given year. Since baptism is the first evidence that disciples are being made (Matthew 28:18–20), it is assumed that, normally, as churches see people come to faith those churches will experience baptisms. Obviously, there are some weaknesses to using baptisms as a sign of evangelistic effectiveness.[10] Despite the limitations, presently it is the best indicator for researchers.

Therefore, a church with two hundred members that baptizes ten people in a given year has a membership to baptism ratio of 20:1. This statistic means that it takes an average of twenty members to make one disciple in one year. A church with a membership of one hundred people that baptizes ten people in a given year has a membership to baptism ratio of 10:1. The lower baptismal ratio assumes a greater evangelistic effectiveness, since it takes fewer people to make one disciple. Since this is a statistic, the size of the congregation is not a problem when comparing large churches with small churches. The baptismal ratio allows us to compare apples to apples, so to speak, when in reality such churches are as different as apples and oranges. For the church with two hundred members to have a baptismal ratio the same as the church of one hundred members, they need to baptize twenty people per year—twice the number.

On average, the churches in my denomination have very poor baptismal ratios. For example, Rainer commented, "We live at a time when it takes on average 86 Southern Baptists per year to bring one person to faith in Jesus Christ."[11] Though there is not a magic number every church should seek to be considered evangelistic, we must realize that something is wrong when the churches in North America are doing a poor job at seeing people baptized.

Our team wanted to know the evangelistic effectiveness of the churches in our study. My assumption was that most house churches are small, and, if they are experiencing baptisms, they should have a low ratio. To my knowledge, no study has ever applied the baptismal ratio to house churches.

In our sample of thirty-three churches, we asked each participant, "When your individual house church gathers for worship and fellowship, what is usually the size of the church present?" Recognizing that many house churches do not keep an official membership record, I assumed that the members of house churches would most likely be present during their congregation's worship gathering. We thus compared worship attendance to baptisms.[12]

The average size of the churches represented in our study

was between fourteen and seventeen people with the average number of baptisms being between four and six in the previous year. In our study, the average membership/attendance to baptism ratio of the house churches ranged from 4.3:1 to 2.3:1. At the high end of the range, these churches were baptizing one person per year for every 4.3 members/attendees. At the low end of the range, for every 2.3 members/attendees, one baptism was witnessed.

The gravity of these numbers should not be passed over casually. *Ratios of this size automatically place these churches among the lowest baptismal ratios in the world. Any traditional congregations manifesting such numbers would automatically be considered the most effective evangelistic churches in North America.*

New Believers Percentage

These congregations had not only outstanding baptismal ratios but they also had outstanding percentages of conversion growth occurring. In the thirty-three churches in our study, the average percentage of new believers in each congregation was between 24 percent and 43 percent.[13] Again, this is a high percentage of new believers in a single congregation. Though these were young churches, just over half had been meeting for four years or more. On average, newer North American churches have lower baptismal ratios and higher percentages of new believers present than older churches. Our research supports this knowledge.

As traditional churches age, usually baptismal ratios increase and the overall percentage of recent converts decreases.[14] But is this also the case in house churches? More research is needed to determine the answer to this question. My initial response is that most house churches will experience the same long-term effects as those experienced by traditional churches, but our data also revealed this situation is not always the case among missional house churches.

The six churches in the study that had been meeting as house churches for ten or more years, reported very low baptismal ratios.[15] The overall ratios ranged from 1.4:1 to 14:1, still some of the best ratios in North America by any scholar's standard (see table below):

Church	Size	Age (yrs)	Baptism Last Year	Ratio Range
1	14–17	13 or more	10+	? – 1.7:1
2	14–17	13 or more	4–6	2.3:1 – 4.3:1
3	14–17	13 or more	1–3	4.7:1 – 17:1
4	14–17	13 or more	1–3	4.7:1 – 17:1
5	26–29	10–12	7–9	2.9:1 – 4.1:1
6	18–21	10–12	7–9	2:1 – 3:1

TABLE 2
**Baptismal Ratio Ranges of Missional House Churches
10 or More Years in Age**

EXTENSION GROWTH

The third type of growth is extension growth. As churches make disciples and plant churches, they experience extension growth. Another characteristic of extension growth is that it is church planting that occurs among people of a similar culture as that of the church planters. Few churches in North America are involved in church planting.

McGavran was correct when he emphasized the importance of church planting by noting, "Thus today's paramount task, opportunity, and imperative in missions is to multiply churches in the increasing numbers of receptive peoples of the earth."[16] Although church growth principles and methods have been taught to North American pastors since the early 1970s, an unhealthy overemphasis on expansion growth has dominated the teachings. Gone is the stress on church planting as a biblical and normative form of growth. It would also be helpful to remember C. Peter Wagner's often quoted statement, "*The single most effective evangelistic methodology under heaven is planting new churches.*"[17]

BRIDGING GROWTH

If extension growth is planting churches among people of a *similar* culture as the church planters, then bridging growth is planting churches among people of a *different* culture than the church planters. The church planters are bridging into a radically different culture with the gospel. For example, a first generation Chinese American congregation that plants a church among the Hispanic community in its city is an example of bridging growth. In North America today, the most urgently needed types of church growth are extension and bridging growth.

Of the 255 churches that took our online survey, 123 had planted at least one church within the past three years. Again, assuming that most missional house churches are new churches *and* that few traditional churches are currently involved in church planting, I set the research parameter low, asking for the number of plants within the past three years.

Our team asked the church leaders, "In the past three years, how many churches has your church planted (started)?" This question could be answered by all thirty-three leaders, regardless of the congregations' ages.[18] Twenty-one of the churches

(64 percent) planted one to three churches; three churches (9 percent) planted ten or more churches.

The average number of churches planted by all thirty-three congregations was surprising. Each of the thirty-three churches, planted an average of four to six new churches. This average represents more than one church plant per church every year for the past three years. Over three years, these churches combined planted approximately 132 to 198 churches. *These numbers alone place such congregations in the highest category of churches planting churches in North America.*

Though I am excited about these initial findings, future research needs to be done to confirm if the churches being planted are by biblical definition actual churches. Until then, I remain hopeful and encouraged by the results of my study.

Evangelism, Assimilation, and Leadership

When studying church growth in house churches, we could have spent much time focusing on a variety of issues. For the purpose of this research, however, our focus was primarily on issues related to methods of evangelism, assimilation, and leadership development. All three of these topics are of great interest to most church leaders.

Methods of Evangelism

Our initial survey[19] asked, "If your church has experienced baptisms within the past year, what means/methods did you use to reach those people from the harvest?" My desire was to offer an open-ended question rather than give a predetermined list of categories from which respondents could select their answers. I wanted to know if a common methodological thread ran through the evangelistic work of these house churches. Did these churches use similar methods to reach those in their communities? If so, what approaches did they use?

According to the churches in our study, the primary means by which these churches believed the Lord worked to bring unbelievers to faith fell into four categories. Though these four categories are not unusual for any church, the percentages of the responses are fascinating.

- Use of Relationships: 67 percent
- Invitation to Church Activities and Use of Relationships: 9 percent
- Community Activities/Special Events: 9 percent
- Invitation to Church Activities: 6 percent[20]

Use of Relationships

For the past several years, and for more reasons than we can discuss here, local church evangelism happens more often in relationship than with complete strangers.[21] Though I suspected that the emphasis placed on relationships that exists in most house churches would obviously affect the churches' methods of evangelism, I was surprised that 67 percent of the leaders surveyed attributed personal relationships as the primary means by which their churches were reaching people with the gospel. By far, this approach dwarfed the other three approaches listed.

I am always concerned when I ask someone about evangelism and they respond with, "Well, I practice lifestyle witnessing," or "Relational evangelism is what our church does." Usually, these answers mean that the person or church attempts to live a good life before unbelievers hoping that either one day an unbeliever will ask about Jesus or that letting their lights shine will automatically bring others to faith. Usually, these answers reveal that evangelism is not taking place. The New Testament clearly teaches that though a godly lifestyle is absolutely necessary, a verbal proclamation of the gospel is necessary as well. For example, the apostle Paul was very clear on this issue when he wrote, "So faith comes from what is heard, and what is heard comes through the message about Christ" (Romans 10:17). The church cannot substitute good deeds for right words and still call it evangelism; both are necessary.

If the above statistics represented house churches in general, I would be deeply concerned that many such churches were not preaching the gospel; however, we were studying those churches that *were* baptizing new believers. Knowing that such churches are emphasizing relationship evangelism supports the argument that it is possible to remain intentional in both our evangelism and our relationships.

Though these churches were not opposed to unbelievers being invited to various church events and gatherings, I did get the impression that they did not see the corporate worship gathering as the primary place when evangelism should occur. One such leader told us that their church places no emphasis on a "come and see" approach to evangelism but rather expects all of the members to "go and tell." Another leader stated, "We encourage that our witnessing be 'as you go' in the local market place to the ends of the earth." Many of these churches would agree with Robert and Julia Banks' statement that "home church members realize that their best opportunities for evangelism lie with people who form part of their everyday contacts."[22]

These churches emphasized the need for their members to

meet unbelievers in their contexts rather than attempting to bring them to a church event. One church saw people coming to faith through "individual disciples reaching out to those they work with or people they meet in the community." Another leader shared that "people within the church reached out to those within their areas of influence—school, work, and so on, and that is how those people were reached."

Sometimes, relational evangelism is accompanied by helping meet peoples' needs. For example, a church leader from Ohio stated, "We simply enter into people's lives. For example, someone in one of our churches knew a lady who just had a baby and was having a difficult time. We began taking meals to her and then started cleaning her messy house. Three months later, she was baptized."

Other times, relational evangelism was tightly connected with family members rather than friends and acquaintances. For example, one leader noted that the parents in their congregations intentionally shared the gospel with their children. He commented, "All of the baptisms in the past year were children of families who had discipled them."

Invitation to Church Activities and Relationships

Only 9 percent of the churches in our study noted that the means by which they saw people come to faith was through a combination of inviting unbelievers to church events and having genuine relationships. I am surprised that this category of methods used was not the most common. More research needs to be conducted to understand the large percentage difference between this category and the means of relationships alone.[23]

Churches that primarily used this means were using invitations to compliment the personal relationships developed. One leader said that this means of seeing people come to faith in

Christ occurred when friends were invited to attend the church activities. Later, these participants were baptized into this local congregation.

Community Activities/Events

Some churches commented that the primary methods whereby people came to faith involved organized activities and events that were open to the public. These churches reached out to their communities through servant-type activities. They sponsored neighborhood parties. One church leader noted that his church started a coffee house for the community. Another congregation developed its own alcohol and drug rehabilitation program. We were also told that when *The Passion of the Christ* was released, one church conducted a general outreach to its local neighborhood.

Invitation to Church Activities

Though few in number, some of the churches in our study saw the use of invitation to church activities as the primary means of experiencing evangelistic growth. For example, one leader said his church would "envelop them [unbelievers] into the intimacy of the church body," and this display of love later resulted in conversions. It is not surprising that few house churches used this method, since it is not highly relational.

Simple Evangelistic Methods

From our study, one thing is clear about missional house churches: their evangelism is simple. To our knowledge, none of the churches in our study had highly sophisticated evangelism programs or activities. In fact, we never heard the word "program" used in our research. Aside from one church leader mentioning that his church taught an Alpha Course, no other survey participant mentioned any commonly used evangelism tool (for example, *Evangelism Explosion, Becoming a Contagious Christian*). This is not to say that such programs are unhelpful, but that the churches in our study simply did not reference them. Phrases such as "relational evangelism," "personal evangelism," "oikos evangelism," and "friendship evangelism" communicated what they were doing to spread the gospel.

The majority of these churches reached people with the gospel primarily through the relationships that God had allowed to develop between church members and those who were unbelievers. Rather than subscribing to an unbiblical form of evangelism that sacrifices the preaching of the gospel for the sake of befriending someone, these churches embrace both and still experience baptisms.

Methods of Assimilation

Assimilation is the term used by church growth researchers describing the process of seeing people become and remain (that is assimilated) fruit-bearing disciples in a local church. While teaching a church growth course in Indianapolis, I had a student who was a Trekie. As soon as he heard me discuss the concept of assimilation, he confessed that all he could think of was the *Star Trek* episodes showing the race of beings known as the Borg who desired to "assimilate" innocent beings into their impersonal, mechanistic system of existence!

Please understand this type of assimilation is not what I am referring to. I wanted to know what was taking place in these churches to make certain that the new believers were remaining actively involved in ministry in their local congregations. I wanted to know what means were being used to make certain that after people were baptized that they were truly incorporated into the local church.

In follow-up surveys, our team asked church leaders, "How does your church know when a believer has a sense of belonging and is thus involved in the life and ministry of the church?" Though it was no surprise that most of these churches had no formal assimilation process (only one church had a covenant class for new believers), the fact that 70 percent of the churches stated that their understanding of assimilation was relational was surprising. Other responses included observable lifestyle changes, repentance and baptism, and a desire to remain with the church even during difficult times.

When we asked church leaders about assimilation, twenty-three of the respondents said their churches knew that a new believer was connected and involved with the church when they witnessed regular "participation," "gift use," and "service." Many times "attendance" was listed in connection with "participation."

For many of these churches the concept of a standardized and formalized membership orientation and accountability system was a foreign, impersonal, and undesired concept. This is not surprising since these churches understand themselves to exist as families. They operate more through their relationships with one another rather than through established written policy.

Though I prefer a relational approach to assimilation, I know from experience that this type of accountability and intimacy requires a level of intentionality that is beyond what is required for just attending church gatherings and taking headcounts. Though our research did not probe deeper into the specific practices of these churches, particularly asking if their assimilation processes worked well, it would have been worthy of study. Is this form of assimilation more effective than what many churches are currently doing through required church membership classes and attendance records? Since most of the churches in the study would agree that the relational approach works best, this is a question for future researchers to determine.[24] I believe that many such churches would benefit from more structure in their assimilation processes, even including an informal membership discussion or full-fledged membership class.

Evidence suggests that the highly relational dynamics in house churches contain the necessary components for effective assimilation. Most house churches, by their very nature, are small groups. Rainer, in his book *High Expectations,* noted that traditional churches that immediately assimilate new believers into their Sunday schools are five times more likely to see those people remain with the church five years later than churches that reach people with the gospel but fail to incorporate them into Sunday school classes.[25] Within another study, Rainer noted that "though the methodologies were many, we found that the most effective assimilation took place where churches were developing disciples through three key foundational elements: expectations, relationships, and involvement."[26]

The majority of missional house churches in our study that used relationships as their primarily means of assimilation were positioned both relationally and structurally to manifest all three characteristics that Rainer observed. It is easy for house churches to be high-expectation churches since they are so relational. Because house churches congregants are connected by a common fellowship rather than an event or place, involvement, accountability, and relationships are natural to their existence.

As life is lived together, no one can be an anonymous or un-involved/inactive church member for very long before someone asks, "What's wrong?" This expression of the body of Christ also offers a high level of accountability to remain faithful to Christ. And of course, it is practically impossible to be a part of a house church and not have several relationships.

LEADERSHIP DEVELOPMENT

Though some within house churches today have wrongly discarded biblical church leadership for an erroneous understanding of the doctrine of the priesthood of the believer, the fact of the matter is that leadership is both biblical *and* extremely significant in churches. Pastors/elders and deacons are clearly part of God's plan for His churches. These biblical positions are not optional. In our research, unfortunately, 15 percent of the respondents noted that elders/pastors were not a part of their congregations, and 61 percent stated that deacons were not included either.

The apostle Paul clearly understood the significance of pastors/elders to the degree that he and Barnabas returned to newly planted churches and appointed elders over them (Acts 14:21–23).[27] In Ephesians he wrote, "And He personally gave some to be apostles, some prophets, some evangelists, some pastors and teachers, for the training of the saints in the work of ministry, to build up the body of Christ, until we all reach unity in the faith and in the knowledge of God's Son, growing into a mature man with a stature measured by Christ's fullness" (Ephesians 4:11–13). In 1 Timothy 3 and in Titus 1, Paul addressed the qualifications for pastors/elders and deacons. In fact, the apostle thought that such leadership was so crucial to the health of the churches that the reason he left Titus in Crete was to "appoint elders in every town" (Titus 1:5). Even a casual reading of Acts 20:17–38 reveals that the apostle Paul understood that leadership was very critical to the health of the Ephesian church because he called together the elders for a meeting in Miletus. I appreciate what Rad Zdero says, "For house churches to be healthy, growing, and multiplying, leaders must be trained adequately to be good shepherds and strategists."[28] It is a tragic problem for churches to discard the biblical teachings regarding pastors/elders and deacons. Thankfully, 85 percent of the respondents in our study said pastors/elders were included in their churches, and 39 percent of the respondents included deacons as well.

Clearly, church leadership includes more than just pastors/elders and deacons. Leadership is influence, and churches have a variety of leaders. In our study, we wanted to know what was working to raise up leaders in general, not specifically pastors/elders and deacons. Additional study in this area of house church leadership is deferred to future researchers.

Raising Up Leaders

Several years ago, Robert Logan and Neil Cole produced a resource entitled *Raising Leaders for the Harvest*.[29] In this material the authors advocated a process to assist with the great need of leadership development, primarily in new churches. Aside from this resource, very few materials address issues related to leadership development in house churches in particular and church planting in general.

While developing the survey instrument, I assumed that the house church leaders being interviewed had some kind of process to develop leaders. This assumption did not prove to be wrong. All of the participants gave evidence of some approach to raising up leaders. Our question was simple, but the responses were not as clear as I would have liked. We asked, "As a house church leader, how are you raising up leaders in your church (steps involved, processes, resources used, etc.)?" We desired to hear from each participant a linear outline such as, "First we do this . . . and second, we do that. . . . and finally we do . . ." What we received, however, was a grouping of concepts that seemed to have no particular linear structure or order.

There were some participants that mentioned formal training—the use of DOVE resources and Life Transformation Groups, and even Aloha Christian Theological Seminary. It was very common for us to hear that these church leaders were significantly involved in coaching, mentoring, and basic discipleship training. Many leaders strongly emphasized training house church leaders through on-the-job training and by modeling desired behaviors before those in training.

Relationships, Relationships, and More Relationships

Though I hoped to hear of a highly structured approach to leadership development, what we discovered was that many of the leaders were using approaches that consisted mainly of training through informal relationships rather than any structured formality. Considering what we know of the importance of relationships in house churches, this discovery was no surprise to us. For many of these leaders, teaching basic disciplines of the Christian faith play a significant role in the raising up church leaders. Some leaders also spoke of watching for the potential leaders to rise to the top and then spending more intentional training time with them. Others identified spiritual gifts within the body and then worked closely with those the Lord was raising up to be leaders. One participant informed us that in his church "leaders just emerge."

The Master Plan of Evangelism

One of the classic texts concerning evangelism is *The Master*

Plan of Evangelism by Robert Coleman.[30] This book has been in print since the 1960s and is still being sold throughout the world. Part of the widespread popularity of the book is its simple thesis. Coleman makes the argument that Jesus' approach to reaching the world with the gospel was a highly simple and reproducible plan that involved pouring Himself into the lives of His disciples over a few years. Those men were then released to reproduce themselves in the lives of others as they made disciples.

For some time, I have been frustrated that North American churches fail to apply Jesus' approach to discipleship/leadership training. If so many people have read Coleman's book, then why are so few people making the necessary application in their churches?

A second, yet related, question is, "Where are the few churches in North America that are applying these principles from the life of Jesus?" Though none of the participants in our study mentioned either the influence of Coleman or his writings on their approach to leadership development, many of these leaders were already following several aspects of what Coleman advocated in his book. As a result of this study, I now believe more churches use this approach to leadership development than I originally assumed.

Is It Working?

Though I assumed that many of these church leaders had some means of training other leaders, I wanted to hear whether they believed their processes were working well. Realizing the limitations of self-assessment type questions, I believed that, given our research constraints, we could still gain some insight into the leadership development occurring among these congregations. We asked the participants to respond to a Likert-type scale (that is strongly agree, agree, uncertain, disagree, strongly disagree) regarding this inquiry, "Please respond accordingly to the following statement: My approach to leadership development is working well." The following table shows the percentage distribution.

Response	Frequency #	Percent
Strongly Agree	8	24%
Agree	19	58%
Uncertain	3	9%
Disagree	1	3%
Strongly Disagree	0	0%
No Response	1	3%
Uncodable	1	3%

TABLE 3
Leadership Development Training Effectiveness

The findings of this question were very surprising. Going into this research, I assumed that the majority of the participants would not have been so confident in their leadership development processes. It was my belief that the "uncertain" category would have been much higher. According to our study, 82 percent of the church leaders believed that their approaches to leadership development were working well. Three participants were uncertain about the effectiveness of their training, and one believed that his approach was not working.

CONCLUSION

God is the One who grows His Church; we are blessed to be a part of that process. There were several surprises when I began to apply traditional church growth statistics to the churches in our study. Though these churches were young, they did have very high percentages of new believers in their fellowships and extremely low baptismal ratios. If the statistics represented by the missional house churches in our study were in the traditional North American churches, then North America would be a radically different place—for the good. According to traditional church growth research, many of the churches in our study were already manifesting the necessary characteristics to facilitate healthy assimilation. Leadership development was primarily based on mentoring, coaching, discipling, and on-the-job training.

Three areas of concern, however, developed from the research. First, more research regarding assimilation is needed. Though I am hopeful, I am not convinced of the long-term effectiveness and benefits of this low-structured approach for highly individualistic societies, such as those found in the West. Second, though there was not much discussion regarding pastors/elders in our study, it is fairly common knowledge that some house churches are so opposed to Western cultural definitions of pastors/elders and deacons that they refuse to have anything to do with such leaders. Churches following this route are not healthy churches, even if they are experiencing significant evangelistic growth and are planting other churches. Finally, the churches in our study were reaching people with the gospel partially because they were highly intentional in their evangelism. What they lacked in organization and evangelistic programs, they made up for in intentionality. Such churches will have to keep their focus, and it will be difficult without some organization and structure.

4

Money and
Missional House Churches

Money often costs too much.

—Ralph Waldo Emerson

Money, money changes everything!

—Cindy Lauper

On December 26, 2004, one of the worst natural disasters occurred. An earthquake in the Indian Ocean caused a tsunami of such a magnitude that approximately 230,000 people lost their lives, making it one of the deadliest disasters in modern history. Numerous countries were affected, and the total amount of destruction was in the billions of dollars. Immediately, the global community began sending aid in the form of workers and money. Thousands of stories poured out of Southeast Asia, tales of horror and loss.

One Sunday soon after the disaster, our pastor read an e-mail he and his wife had received earlier that week from a missionary couple working in Southeast Asia. They had been close friends for some time and continued their long distance relationship. The e-mail was an update of what was going on in their region of the world since the devastating event. They asked for prayer and gave a specific address to which relief assistance could be mailed.

After reading the e-mail, our pastor asked the church to consider sending a love offering directly to this couple, since they would know how to spend the money in their context. It was decided that before we ended our Sunday gathering we would determine a dollar amount to send.

After worship time, we were again asked what amount we should send to the missionaries working with the tsunami victims. After a moment of silence from the approximately thirty believers present, one sister said the amount that came to her mind was $2,000. With little discussion and no disagreement, the church decided immediately that this was of the Lord and sent the amount to our brother and sister ministering in Southeast Asia.

I do not share this story to boast, though I do boast in the Lord that we were able to provide such an offering. I share this story as an example of the use of finances in many house churches. Our small group of believers gave more to missions on that particular Sunday than many churches with hundreds of members give to missions over an entire year. In fact, when I was a member of this particular church, we were blessed to give over $10,000 to missions one year. In many house churches, money is rarely an issue of debate and division, as it has been in many traditional churches throughout North America.

When I was a minister with one traditional church, I found myself living with a frustration related to our budget. Seventy-six percent of our budget was given to salaries and the expenses related to our physical facility. Although we spent so much in these two areas, our growth was slow at best, we were not raising up leaders, and our facility was falling apart. My frustration increased when it took us several months to recover financially from the few thousand dollars we spent on vacation Bible school during the summer.

As I speak to people about house churches, one of the first topics of discussion regards the issue of money. I write this chapter because of this popular interest and also because of what some house churches are doing with their monies. For example, Jim Melon wrote, "Over the last 13 years we have been able to deploy approximately $1M away from building payments and salaries towards benevolence and missions. We have helped plant over 450 churches in India, influence our community, and save a life through benevolence giving."[1]

TITHES AND OFFERINGS?

Many house churches unfortunately, do not regularly collect tithes and offerings. I am troubled by this since I believe that the Scriptures are clear on the need for such a practice. Of the churches in our study, seventeen of the leaders (about 52 percent) reported that their churches regularly collected tithes and offerings. A limitation of our study was that we did not define *regularly* in our survey. Some of the churches offered us reasons why they did not regularly collect money: "We don't want to offend anyone," and "The tithe was under the law; now under Christ we freely give offerings as needed."

How the Money Is Used

Rad Zdero has clearly revealed that house churches in general use their finances in a multitude of ways. In his book *The Global House Church Movement,* he stated,

> There are different practices among house churches concerning church bank accounts, tax deductible donations, and tithing. There are advantages and disadvantages to each of these items. Some house churches do not incorporate any of these elements, but rather use money solely for mutual support within the house church as the need arises and in assisting the poor. Money, thus, flows directly from the giver to getter, and bypasses middle agencies like the government and denominational finance departments. Others incorporate all three elements and, in that way, function like traditional churches, except that the money is not spent on expensive programs, paying rent or paying for the church building program, or supporting professional clergy. Instead, they funnel their money to the poor, for resources to be used within the house church and/or network, and in the support of house church planters and mobile network overseers. There are also house churches that fall somewhere between these two ends of the financial management spectrum.[2]

In our study, there were house churches that met in rented facilities and had various costs involved with rental property, and some had administrative costs such as office supplies, mailing expenses, leadership training, and financial support for their elders. The majority of the churches, however, used their finances for missions and benevolence (meeting both community needs and needs within the church). One church leader noted that his church usually gave 70–80 percent of their finances to missions and to meet needs. Within missional house churches, it is not uncommon to hear of such large quantities (including higher percentages) being given to these two areas.

TO BE PAID OR NOT TO BE PAID

The issue of church leaders receiving financial support is a hot-button topic in many house churches. On one hand, some churches are adamantly opposed to anyone receiving any financial support from the church body. John White, in his article "Financing Ministry," commented on this struggle in house church life.

> Martin Luther once remarked that the church is like a drunken horseman. Prop him up on one side, and he falls off on the other. Nowhere is this truer than with church finance. In the traditional church environment, there have been many problems with money. Perhaps the most pervasive is that the concept of salaried church staff has resulted in perpetuating the clergy/laity divide.
>
> As a result of reacting to the abuses, many in the house church movement are in danger of "falling off

the other side." The thinking is that if there are no full-time workers and everyone is a tentmaker, we will be kept safe from the development of "house church clergy."[3]

Though White believes there will be times when tentmakers are a necessary option, he noted that since the harvest is ripe, full-time workers are also needed. Continuing on, he wrote, "Releasing thousands of full-time apostles (skilled and gifted house church planters) is by far the best strategy for starting a million house churches in the U.S. in this decade."[4]

On the other hand, other churches see that it as a regular part of church life is giving a salary (part-time or full-time) to their leaders. From our research, by far the most common approach, however, has been for churches *not* to provide a regular offering to their pastors. If they regularly provided an income to anyone, it was usually to the leaders who were planting other churches and overseeing the networks of house churches.

Steve Atkerson's perspective of financial support of local church pastors was a common view we encountered. Atkerson is opposed to the church employing pastors. However, he believes that "as with Paul, elders can receive 'good things' shared voluntarily with them by the saints to whom they minister, but elders are primarily to supply their own needs by working hard in the secular world."[5]

In his article "Financing the Work," Neil Cole listed three categories of individuals who should be receive support. Reasoning from the Scriptures, he delineated these categories: 1) apostles, 2) widows, and 3) elders.[6] Citing 1 Corinthians 9, Cole commented that the apostles had the right to be supported by the churches, even though Paul on different occasions gave up that right. Second, Cole referenced 1 Timothy 5:3–16 as addressing the possible need for the churches to regularly support older widows. He continued on to mention Paul's guidelines for supporting elders in the churches (1 Timothy 5:17–18). Offering his commentary, he noted:

> I am in favor of giving honor and double honor to godly elders who shepherd, mentor, and teach the churches. However, I have a hard time interpreting "double honor" as a full-time salary and benefits. We have come up with the word "honorarium" based on this expression in the New Testament. When we present a speaker with a financial token of appreciation, I actually think we are closer to Paul's intent in this passage.
>
> To be fair, Paul does refer to a "worker worthy of his wages" which is a quote from the Old Testament and from Jesus as well; however, it is probably in reference to paying for a day's hire rather than a yearly salary. We should definitely be generous in sharing all good things with those who teach us (Gal. 6:6), but the goal is always the strengthening of the church, not the sapping of her strength.[7]

In our study, only a couple network leaders actually received regular financial support from the churches. Both of these men had connections with denominations and had no secular form of employment. At least six of the participants in our study stated that their churches regularly gave financial support to their individual house church pastors. The majority of the network leaders and individual house church pastors (which sometimes included the same leaders overseeing the network) did not receive regular financial support from the churches. Cole's comments reflect those of many house church pastors: "In the context of organic churching, where churches are intentionally smaller, more intimate, and rapidly reproducing, there is not a need to pay someone to pastor. The bar for ministry is down low enough that it is easy to shepherd 10 to 20 people without needing to be paid to do so. In such a context, the whole body is more easily mobilized to serve, and ministry is not as dependent on a single professional leader."[8]

BIBLICAL EVIDENCE

The Scriptures speak clearly regarding finances and church life. The remaining section of this chapter examines these passages. I have chosen to spend a substantial amount of time on this topic because of its relevance to church life in general and the missional house churches in particular.

It is my conviction that though the tithe was established in the Torah (even before the law was given, Genesis 14:20; 28:22), it should be a starting point for followers of Jesus and should be given out of love and not compulsion. I do not find New Testament evidence that this regular giving ever ceased. Christians should regularly give *at least* 10 percent of their gross income (in a cash-based society). Those who advocate giving when a need arises are usually not making themselves open to the needs around them.

Beginning with the Old and New Testament concept of tithing, this section examines who in the churches should receive financial support and other ways in which the churches' monies should be used.

OLD TESTAMENT TITHING

The word *tithe* means a "tenth," or "tenth part." The word for tithe occurs thirty-two times in the Old Testament.[9] The first two references to the tithe are found in Genesis and relate to Abram and Jacob, centuries before the law was given. After returning from battle, Abram is blessed by Melchizedek, king of Salem and "priest to God Most High." In response, Abram gave Melchizedek a tenth of the spoils of the battle (Genesis 14:17–20). Years later, Jacob had a dream in which the Lord made a covenant with Jacob. Upon awaking, Jacob made a vow to return to the Lord a tenth of all he received from the Lord (Genesis 28:22).

Centuries later, Moses wrote that "every tenth of the land's produce, grain from the soil or fruit from the trees, belongs to the Lord; it is holy to the Lord. . . . Every tenth animal from the herd or flock . . . will be holy to the Lord" (Leviticus 27:30–32). From this passage, it is easy to see that the tithe of all of the people of Israel was holy and belonged to the Lord. When the Israelites settled in the Promised Land, it was clearly stated that the Levites were not to receive any inheritance of the land; the Lord was their inheritance. They were, however, to receive "the tenth that the Israelites present to the Lord as a contribution for their inheritance" (Numbers 18:24). The Lord commanded that the holy tithe be given to those who served near the altar and the ark of the covenant. In a section of Deuteronomy addressing the need for the people to bring their offerings and tithes to a designated area, Moses wrote that they were to "be careful not to neglect the Levite, as long as you live in your land" (Deuteronomy 12:19). Also, in some instances, the people were permitted to eat of their tithe and to share part of the tithe with the sojourner and needy (Deuteronomy 12:1–18; 14:22–29; 18:1–4; 26:12–15).

The other prominent Old Testament passage addressing the tithe is Malachi 3:8–10. After the Israelites were permitted to return to the land following their exile in captivity, the prophet reminded them of their disobedience to the Lord. They were robbing God by withholding their tithes and offerings. The prophet called the people to repent and to watch for the return of God's blessings.

In these Old Testament passages, it is clear that Abraham and Jacob practiced tithing over four hundred years before the Mosaic law was established. And, though the people themselves, the sojourner, and the needy at times could benefit from the tithe, the primary recipients were the Levites who served at the Tent of the Meeting. To withhold a tithe was tantamount to stealing from the Lord. Carpenter's words provide an excellent summary as to the meaning of the tithe: "No institution in Israel, including tithing, existed merely to carry out a political, economic, or humanitarian function. By giving the tithe the Israelites were declaring solemnly that they were giving a portion back to the Lord who had prospered them (cf. Deut. 26:10–15). By giving the tithe they also recognized the validity of the priests' and Levites' role as God's representatives and acknowledged their right to receive support for the spiritual service they performed on the people's behalf."[10]

New Testament Tithing

The New Testament has few verses addressing the tithe. Despite the paucity of words, it does have much to say about this topic. First, though Jesus only referenced the tithe a couple of times, He did not discard the tithe. In one of His most heated encounters with the scribes and Pharisees, he rebuked them not because they practiced tithing but because they had neglected the "more important matters of the law—justice, mercy, and faith" (Matthew 23:23). Immediately following this condemnation, He stated, "These things should have been done without neglecting the others" (Matthew 23:23; cf. Luke 11:42). In other words, the religious leaders were not doing enough. They emphasized one aspect of a godly life while neglecting the other, and Jesus said they needed both.

Often, 2 Corinthians 9:1–13 is listed as a New Testament text that implies the concept of tithing. Paul was preparing the Corinthian Church for the arrival of a team (including himself) to obtain an offering from them to give to other believers in need. Though this passage teaches us about cheerful and abundant giving, it is not addressing the concept of tithing but rather a particular offering to be collected and sent to Jerusalem.

The final New Testament passage that indirectly addresses the notion of the tithe actually refers to Abraham in the book of Genesis. Hebrews 7 discusses the priestly order of Melchizedek and then makes a comparison of Jesus to this mysterious Old Testament figure. After establishing the fact that Abraham gave a tithe of the spoils to Melchizedek (vv. 1–3) and was also blessed by him, the writer makes the point that Melchizedek (the superior) blessed Abraham (the inferior, v. 7). Then arguing that the Levitical priesthood is inferior to the order of Melchizedek, the author stated, "And in a sense Levi himself, who receives tithes, has paid tithes through Abraham, for he was still within his forefather when Melchizedek met him" (vv. 9–10). The climax of this chapter is the fact that the Levitical priesthood was not perfect, but Jesus is "in the order of Melchizedek" (v. 11) and is the perfect High Priest (v. 17–19; 8:1), "the guarantee of a better covenant" (v. 22).

So what does this passage have to do with the practice of tithing today? Though the primary purpose of this passage is not to address the practice of tithing, there are several points to deduce from Hebrews 7. First, Israel was required to give a tithe to the Levites, even though the writer of Hebrews makes it clear that the Levites were inferior to Melchizedek. Second, Abraham, who was greater than Aaron and the Levites, was blessed by Melchizedek and offered a tithe to this priest of the Most High God, thus showing his own inferiority. Finally, since Jesus is after the order of Melchizedek, how much more should believers offer *at least* a tithe of their means to the Lord? The New Testament does not advocate the discarding of the tithe but rather uses it as *a beginning point*, since all that we have is from God and belongs to Him.

GIVING TO LEADERS

Though it has already been noted that the Old Testament advocated that the Levites received and benefited from the tithe, the New Testament also addressed the issue of giving to church leaders.

APOSTOLIC LEADERS

In Matthew 10, Jesus sent out the Twelve with the following instructions: "Don't take the road leading to other nations, and don't enter any Samaritan town. Instead, go to the lost sheep of the house of Israel. As you go, announce this: 'The kingdom of heaven has come near.' Heal the sick, raise the dead, cleanse those with skin diseases, drive out demons. You have received free of charge; give free of charge. Don't take along gold, silver, or copper for your money-belts. Don't take a traveling bag for the road, or an extra shirt, sandals, or a walking stick, for the worker is worthy of his food" (Matthew 10:5–10).

Just as the disciples had freely received the blessings of the Lord, they were in turn to respond by freely being a blessing to others. The Lord's instruction capitalized on the hospitality of the day (Luke 9:4). It was common for someone to offer hospitality to a traveler, a practice that extended all the way back to the days of Abraham (Genesis 18:1–8; 19:1–3). Later, Jesus sent out seventy others on another mission trip. His instructions were similar: "Don't carry a money-bag, traveling bag, or sandals; don't greet anyone along the road. Whatever house you enter, first say, 'Peace to this household.' If a son of peace is there, your peace will rest on him; but if not, it will return to you. Remain in the same house, eating and drinking what they offer, for the worker is worthy of his wages. Don't be moving from house to house" (Luke 10:4–7).

It is clear from the context of these two passages (Matthew 9 and Luke 10) that the "wages" mentioned are a place to bed and food to eat. It is also worthy of attention that Jesus specifically told his disciples to remain in one house rather than venturing from house to house, possibly to avoid the image that they were peddlers of religious teachings.

The apostle Paul referenced Jesus' words that "the laborer is worthy of his wages" in 1 Timothy 5:18. Since the context of Paul's words relates to honoring elders, I will address it later.

TENTMAKING

Tentmakers are those involved in church planting practices while simultaneously supporting themselves with a secular form of employment.[11] J. Christy Wilson, Jr., who has been hailed as the father of the contemporary tentmaking movement, noted that the Apostle Paul best portrays a tentmaker. According to Wilson, "The apostle Paul, who thus supported himself, was the greatest missionary who ever lived. In Acts 18:1–5 we read, 'Paul . . . came to Corinth and found a certain Jew named Aquila, . . . lately come from Italy, with his wife Priscilla, . . . And because he was of the same craft, he abode with them, and wrought: for by their occupation they were tentmakers. And he . . . persuaded the Jews and the Greeks . . . that Jesus was Christ.'"[12]

LUKAN NARRATIVE

Aside from the just mentioned Acts 18:1–5 passage, there is one other passage in Acts that offers substantial evidence for the apostle's tentmaking paradigm, Acts 20:32–35. The setting was in Miletus; the audience was the elders of the Ephesian church. Since Paul was in a hurry to arrive in Jerusalem before Pentecost, he sailed past Ephesus and called for the elders to meet him. In this farewell address, Paul's last words to the church leaders included his usual admonition to imitate his lifestyle:

> And now I commit you to God and to the message of His grace, which is able to build you up and to give you an inheritance among all who are sanctified. I have not coveted anyone's silver or gold or clothing. You yourselves know that these hands have provided for my needs, and for those who were with me. In

every way I've shown you that by laboring like this,
it is necessary to help the weak and to keep in mind
the words of the Lord Jesus, for He said, "It is more
blessed to give than to receive."

By manifesting a healthy work ethic, Paul avoided the ac-
cusation of avarice and truly showed the example of a servant
leader, without giving the wrong impression.

CORINTHIAN CORRESPONDENCE

There are several Corinthian passages that offer evidence for
and explanation of Paul's tentmaking practice. In 1 Corinthians
4:12, Paul made the passing statement that he was one who
worked with his own hands.[13] In chapter 9, the apostle made a
very clear declaration that he indeed had the right to provender
and drink from the Corinthians (v. 4). But he abdicated this
right so as to not hinder the spread of the gospel (v. 12), and
he considered it a reward to preach the gospel without charge
(v. 18). He made himself a slave to all so that he might "win
more people" (v. 19) and show his desire to "become all things to
all people, so that I may by all means save some" (v. 22).

THESSALONIAN CORRESPONDENCE

Paul maintained his tentmaking practice while in
Thessalonica. In 1 Thessalonians 2:9, Paul reminded the Church
that he and this team labored "night and day" to not burden
them. Later, in his second letter to the Church, he echoed his
Corinthian abdication, in conjunction with the problem that
the Thessalonian Church had with members who were unwilling
to work. He wrote:

Now we command you, brothers, in the name of our
Lord Jesus Christ, to keep away from every brother
who walks irresponsibly and not according to the
tradition received from us. For you yourselves know
how you must imitate us: we were not irresponsible
among you; we did not eat anyone's bread free of
charge; instead, we labored and toiled, working
night and day, so that we would not be a burden to
any of you. It is not that we don't have the right to
support, but we did it to make ourselves an example
to you so that you would imitate us. In fact, when we
were with you, this is what we commanded you: "If
anyone isn't willing to work, he should not eat." For
we hear that there are some among you who walk
irresponsibly, not working at all, but interfering with
the work of others. Now we command and exhort
such people, by the Lord Jesus Christ, that quietly
working, they may eat their own bread.[14]

But Not Always Tentmaking

Though it is easy to assume that the apostle Paul received
support solely from his tentmaking abilities, this assumption is
not entirely correct. Tentmaking was a significant and regular part
of the apostle's ministry; however, it is clear from the Scriptures
that he received support from at least two other sources: other
churches (2 Corinthians 11:9; Philippians 4:15–20) and individuals (Acts 16:15).[15] F. F. Bruce's comments are helpful "He
supported himself, and his companions where necessary, by his
'tent-making.' Many rabbis practiced a trade so as to be able to
impart their teaching without charge. Paul scrupulously main-

tained this tradition as a Christian preacher, partly as a matter of principle, partly by way of example to his converts, and partly to avoid giving his critics any opportunity to say that his motives were mercenary. When, however, hospitality was spontaneously offered [for example, Lydia] . . . he gladly accepted it: it would have been ungracious to refuse."[16]

ELDERS

Peter referred to himself as both an apostle (1 Peter 1:1) and a "fellow elder" (1 Peter 5:1). According to Luke (Acts 20) and Paul's writings to Timothy and Titus (1 Timothy 3 and Titus 1), the elders apparently were local overseers/pastors of the churches.

On the one hand, it seems as if elders did receive financial gifts from the churches. For example, Peter wrote: "Therefore, as a fellow elder and witness to the sufferings of the Messiah, and also a participant in the glory about to be revealed, I exhort the elders among you: shepherd God's flock among you, not overseeing out of compulsion but freely, according to God's will; *not for the money* but eagerly; not lording it over those entrusted to you, but being examples to the flock" (1 Peter 5:1–3, emphasis mine). If money was unavailable and not given in certain circumstances, then why did the apostle bother mentioning it if it was not assumed to be on the minds of his readers?

The most common passage to which many refer is 1 Timothy 5:17–18. In referencing the Old Testament and Jesus, Paul wrote, "The elders who are good leaders should be considered worthy of an ample honorarium, especially those who work hard at preaching and teaching. For the Scripture says: You must not muzzle an ox that is threshing grain, and, The laborer is worthy of his wages."

This reference to not muzzling the ox is taken from Deuteronomy 25:4. The Israelites were told to allow their oxen to eat as they went about their daily labors of threshing out the grain. If the animals became hungry, they were not to be restrained from taking a bite of grain. Later, in 1 Corinthians 9:9–11, the apostle Paul offered his commentary on this passage in the context of informing the Corinthians of the apostolic rights that he abdicated in order to become all things to all men to win people to Christ: "For it is written in the law of Moses, Do not muzzle an ox while it treads out the grain. Is God really concerned with oxen? Or isn't He really saying it for us? Yes, this is written for us, because he who plows ought to plow in hope, and he who threshes should do so in hope of sharing the crop. If we have sown spiritual things for you, is it too much if we reap material things from you?"

The same Paul who wrote this Corinthian text also wrote 1 Timothy. So, it is appropriate that Paul's correspondence to Timothy be understood in light of his Corinthian interpretation. Therefore, it is clear that the elders were permitted to receive material support from the churches.

We must not read our contemporary practices into the text and assume that the apostle and Jesus had our notion of a "salary" or "package" in mind as they addressed the issue of the apostles and elders receiving financial support from the churches. Though I am not opposed to churches providing salaries and packages to their ministers, the "ample honorarium" (1 Timothy 5:17) was probably closer to our practice of a stipend or honorarium than to an annual salary (cf. Galatians 6:6). Also, Paul's reference to Jesus' words, "The laborer is worthy of his wages" (1 Timothy

5:18; cf. Matthew 10:10; Luke 10:7) was originally spoken in the context of Jesus sending out preachers who were in need of food and lodging (see above discussion).

When Paul was in Miletus, he called for the elders of the church in Ephesus to meet with him for his farewell address. Toward the end of this address, he reminded them of his example regarding his willingness to work to support both himself and his team: "I have not coveted anyone's silver or gold or clothing. You yourselves know that these hands have provided for my needs, and for those who were with me. In every way I've shown you that, by laboring like this, it is necessary to help the weak and to keep in mind the words of the Lord Jesus, for He said, 'It is more blessed to give than to receive'" (Acts 20:33–35).

When this passage is taken in conjunction with Paul's writings to Timothy while he was in Ephesus, we gain a better understanding of the relationship between the Ephesian elders and financial compensation. Though Paul was not opposed to them receiving some provision from the church, he believed that an example of working to provide for his own needs was a better example and one he was willing to set before the Ephesian believers.

BENEVOLENCE

From our study, many of the churches give a substantial amount of their finances to benevolence. This need usually took the form of assisting with material needs first within the church and then in the community. Next to missions, virtually every leader said his church gives to benevolence.

OLD TESTAMENT

We do not have to look very far to gain an Old Testament perspective of the commands of the Lord to the Israelites regarding benevolent-type assistance. Throughout the Old Testament, God always had a special concern for the poor, the widow, the orphan, and the foreigner (Exodus 22:22; Deuteronomy 14:29; 24:19; 26:12; Psalm 10:14; 68:5; Zechariah 7:10). This compassion should come as no surprise to us, for God is the God of love and comes to rescue those in need. For example, Ezekiel reminded Jerusalem of her abandonment at birth, but adoption by the Lord (Ezekiel 16:1–7). The Old Testament is also not shy on passages that reveal God's love for the poor and how His people are to assist with their needs (Exodus 23:11; Leviticus 19:10; 23:22; Deuteronomy 15:11; Psalm 41:1; Proverbs 14:31; 19:17; 31:20; Isaiah 58:7; 61:1; Jeremiah 22:16).

NEW TESTAMENT

The Old Testament patterns for the relationship of God's people to the needy are carried over into the New Testament and applied to the Church. There was ongoing food assistance for the widows in the Jerusalem congregation. As the church continued to grow, a complaint emerged from the Hellenistic Jews against the Hebraic Jews regarding the daily food distribution. Rather than seeing this as an insignificant issue, the church continued this ministry by selecting seven men so the Twelve could devote themselves to prayer and preaching (Acts 6:1–7).

James, writing about the necessity of a follower of Jesus being both a hearer and doer of the Word, makes a one-sentence comment about true religion, revealing the apostolic Church's concern for widows and orphans. He stated, "Pure and undefiled religion before our God and Father is this: to look after orphans and widows in their distress and to keep oneself unstained by the world" (James 1:27).

By far the most extensive New Testament passage related to the necessity of churches caring for widows is 1 Timothy 5:3–16. Paul offered several detailed instructions regarding the benevolent ministry of the church toward their widows. The church had an official support list for widows over the age of sixty.

Throughout Church history, Christians have always helped the poor. This was also true in the apostolic Church. Paul was reminded to "remember the poor" (Galatians 2:10) throughout his missionary journeys. When Agabus predicted a severe famine in the Roman world (Acts 11:28), the church in Antioch sent assistance to the brothers living in Judea (Acts 11:29). Paul requested that the Corinthian church send assistance to the Jerusalem church in their time of need (1 Corinthians 16:1–4). When Paul wrote to the Roman believers, he commented on the Gentile churches assisting the believers in Jerusalem: "Now, however, I am traveling to Jerusalem to serve the saints; for Macedonia and Achaia were pleased to make a contribution to the poor among the saints in Jerusalem" (Romans 15:25–26).

One other example of the apostolic Church clearly providing for its needy members is found early in the book of Acts. It is here that we have the best example of what true biblical fellowship looks like. The church was preaching the gospel and ministering to one another. Luke recorded, "For there was not a needy person among them, because all those who owned lands or houses sold them, brought the proceeds of the things that were sold, and laid them at the apostles' feet. This was then distributed to each person as anyone had a need" (Acts 4:34–35). This was not some example of Christian communism but rather the body of Christ so much in love with Jesus and each other that they were willing to part with their own possessions to assist a needy brother or sister.

CONCLUSION

The issue of money in the church has always been a sensitive one. However, most house churches do not see money as a potential point of friction as some traditional churches do. In our study, the majority of missional house churches that regularly collect tithes and offerings tended to use most of those resources for mission work and benevolence. Some churches did use a small proportion for administrative work or to periodically rent a larger place for their network to meet. A few of the churches provided their pastoral leadership with financial income.

5

The Future of Missional House Churches

Prediction is very difficult,
especially of the future.

—Niels Bohr

Change is the law of life.
And those who look only to the past or present
are certain to miss the future.

—John F. Kennedy

Jesus Christ is the same
yesterday, today, and forever.

—Hebrews 13:8

The world has seen its share of prognosticators and their failed predictions. I, therefore, do not want to predict the future of house churches in too great of detail. Regarding the future, one thing is highly probable: house churches will continue to exist until the Lord's return. Just as I hesitate to make many definitive assumptions about the future of house churches in North America, those who are quick to write off the house church and its possible influence on societal transformation should also not be quick to make assumptions. Consider the following "famous last words":

- "This 'telephone' has too many shortcomings to be seriously considered as a means of communication. The device is inherently of no value to us." (Western Union internal memo, 1876)
- "The wireless music box has no imaginable commercial value. Who would pay for a message sent to nobody in particular?" (David Sarnoff's associates in response to his urgings for investment in the radio in the 1920s)
- "We don't like their sound, and guitar music is on the way out." (Decca Recording Company, rejecting the Beatles, 1962)
- "So we went to Atari and said, 'Hey, we've got this amazing thing, even built with some of your parts, and what do you think about funding us? Or we'll give it to you. We just want to do it. Pay our salary, we'll come work for you.' And they said, 'No.' So then we went to Hewlett-Packard, and they said, 'Hey, we don't need you. You haven't got through college yet.'" (Apple Computer Inc.

founder Steve Jobs, on attempts to get Atari and H-P interested in his and Steve Wozniak's personal computer)

- "Drill for oil? You mean drill into the ground to try and find oil? You're crazy." (Drillers whom Edwin L. Drake tried to enlist in his project to drill for oil in 1859)
- "No flying machine will ever fly from New York to Paris." (Orville Wright)
- "Airplanes are interesting toys but of no military value." (Marechal Ferdinand Foch, Professor of Strategy, Ecole Superieure de Guerre)[1]

In our research, we wanted to hear from the hearts of those leaders who were serving in missional house churches scattered across this continent regarding their thoughts on the future of such churches. One of the last questions that our team asked the leaders was, "In general, what do you think will become of house churches in North America in the next ten years?"

WHAT MISSIONAL HOUSE CHURCH LEADERS ARE SAYING

The house church leaders in our study have great hopes for the future of house churches. Usually the immediate response we received when we inquired about the future was that this form of church life would continue to grow. We constantly heard descriptions projecting "explosive growth" and "great growth" of these churches. Some spoke of the multiplication of these churches and the growth of the House Church Movement in particular. One thing is certain: these missional house church leaders do not see the demise of house churches in North America anytime soon.

A few leaders, however, shared their concerns that some of the churches will institutionalize and become like their traditional counterparts. Others believed that it will become a normative expression of church life on this continent.

If history is the best predictor of the future, then house church expressions will become increasingly accepted in North America. I have curiously observed a phenomenon in North America that I refer to as the "West Coast Creep." Though this phenomenon is predominately observed in pop culture, I have also noticed its presence in the Church, especially over the past twenty to thirty years. The "creep" can be summed up in the following statement: As goes the West Coast, so goes the rest of the country.

What is seen today on the West Coast will eventually creep the United States all the way to the Atlantic. Clearly, this is not a universal law, and there are many East Coast and even Midwest influences also shape and change the country. However, this phenomenon can be observed at least over the past few decades.

For example, in the late 1970s and 1980s, the method-ologies, structures, organizations, and leadership styles of some California churches were avant-guard for their time—and con-troversial. Donald McGavran started teaching church growth principles to U.S. pastors in Pasadena in the early 1970s. Rick Warren and Bob Logan were using many nontraditional ap-proaches in the ministry that resulted in criticism and opposition from established church leaders. Within fifteen years, rightly or wrongly, however, others across the nation had embraced many of their philosophies, missiologies, and methods. What was once troublesome and problematic became the norm in many circles.

Just think of the number of "purpose-driven" churches scattered across the continent today as compared to a decade ago.

In the mid-1990s, I heard a nationally recognized leader in church growth studies say that the "cell church phenomena" was predominately a West Coast trend and that no one could point him to an effective cell church on the eastern side of the Mississippi.[2] Within ten years, however, numerous church plants in this country are cell churches in structure and function. The cell model has now become a regular expression among many new churches, and many older churches have transitioned to cell or cell-like structures.

Based on these two examples, I can only speculate that house churches will become even more popular across the United States as time continues. As noted in this study, missional house churches are already scattered across the country, including many on the West coast that did not make it into our study. What is even more interesting is that current influential house church leaders originate from several regions—the West Coast, East Coast, and the Bible belt.

In the late 1970s, Dick Scoggins and Jim Frost planted networks of house churches in New England. These men later developed the Fellowship of Church Planters. Neil Cole, who started the Awakening Chapel movement, began in California in the 1990s and now, primarily through Church Multiplication Associates, has much influence across the country in planting house churches.[3] Tony and Felicity Dale, in Texas, have been involved with the ongoing National House Church Conference and *House2House* magazine. In the Southeast, Steve Atkerson has been promoting house churches with his conferences through the New Testament Restoration Foundation and the publication *Toward a House Church Theology.*

Attitudes of Traditional Churches

From the perspective of many traditional churches and denominations on this continent, there are at least three general attitudes toward house churches that will continue long into the future. These attitudes usually manifest themselves as acceptance, opposition, or apathy.

Acceptance

Even within North America, some denominations have seen the importance of planting missional house churches. For example, along with several other models of church, the Dallas Baptist Association's website states: "The DBA seeks to assist churches and church planters in starting target specific congregations. Some of the various types of Church Planting Models include Traditional, Multicultural, Special Interest, *House Churches*, Cultural Specific, Contemporary, Seeker Sensitive, Language, Emerging Generation, Multi-housing Churches, Postmodern, Bi-vocational Homogeneous, and Country Western."[4]

Within our study, some churches were affiliated with a national denomination: Southern Baptist, Grace Brethren, Disciples of Christ, or Church of Christ. Whether the reason for accepting and encouraging such expressions of the body of Christ is theological, strategic, pragmatic, or any combination of the three, several well-established churches and denominations support of house churches.

Opposition

Unfortunately, Church history is replete with examples of Christians in conflict with other Christians. Megachurch pastor

Larry Kreider noted in his book *House Church Networks*, "Over the course of history, new moves of God have often persecuted the next wave of God's Spirit. Early reformer Martin Luther persecuted the Anabaptists and had them placed in prison. I have heard some of my Assembly of God pastor friends lament that they persecuted the Charismatic movement of the 1960s and 1970s."[5]

Despite the growing acceptance of house churches in North America, unhealthy opposition and even hostility exist. I clearly recognize that there are certain practices in many house churches that are unhealthy practices and need to be addressed by the larger body of Christ. Though I have addressed some of those issues in this book (for example, discarding pastors, isolation from other churches, etc.), I do not advocate an ungodly approach to challenging and correcting our brothers and sisters. Though conflict will continue among those in the household of faith, we must remember that we are to engage one another with the proper spirit that reflects a Christ-like manner.

Where right doctrine and right practice exist, we should support and encourage house churches, even if they are not reflecting a model of church life based on our cultural preferences. Kreider, who served as a megachurch pastor, is quick to remind the Church not to repeat the errors of our past. To the extent that right doctrine and practice are present I agree with Kreider. "So how should those of us called to serve with community churches and mega-churches respond to house church networks that emerge in our community? Let's welcome them, reach out to them and offer them help to succeed. . . . Let's allow the house church networks to grow up alongside the community churches and the mega-churches in our communities. We need to see ourselves as a part of the regional church the Lord is raising up in these times."[6]

We asked missional house church leaders, "What are the greatest challenges you face as a house church leader?" Though this topic is addressed in detail below, thankfully the opposition from established churches is not a major issue for these leaders. Some leaders, however, did speak of their struggles with those who oppose what they are doing. For example, we did receive a few responses noting, "Many think we are not a legitimate expression of the body of Christ" and that they were experiencing "persecution from organized religious institutions."

Apathy

The third response of established churches toward house churches, and probably the most popular, is that of apathy. Many churches have no strong emotions toward house churches. Though they may consider this expression of the body of Christ as something strange, foreign, or less than a church, indifference abounds. This attitude of apathy is not necessarily a bad thing; traditional churches have concerns and passions of their own and choose neither to promote nor oppose house churches.

Members

As house churches in general continue to grow and multiply across North America, who will become the members of such churches?[7] Unfortunately, as with the majority of North American churches, most house churches will continue to come into existence and grow through Christians leaving other churches and not from new believers coming out of the harvest.

Though transfer growth (the shuffling of the saints from congregation to congregation) is not always bad, it is not biblical church growth.[8]

A major issue facing future North American house churches is that many of them will be no different (missionally-speaking) than the majority of the traditional churches on this continent. As nonmissional church members leave traditional churches, they will plant or become part of house churches that are evangelistically anemic.

The future membership in North America's house churches will generally fall into the following four categories: hurting Christians, new-experience Christians, anti-establishment Christians, and new believers.

HURTING CHRISTIANS

There are many hurting Christians on this continent. For whatever reasons, many believers who have had significant involvement in traditional church life have been wounded psychologically, sexually, emotionally, spiritually, or physically, and many times a combination of these areas. Many have been hurt by other Christians and have "given up" on the established church. Some see house churches as the answer to their problems, and many house churches see themselves primarily as a place for such hurting believers. As many believers turn to house churches for therapeutic reasons, house churches will continue to increase.

NEW-EXPERIENCE CHRISTIANS

The consumerism and individualism that pervades western culture and that has been embraced by much of the western

Church will affect the future of North American house churches. Christians, tired of traditional expressions of the faith, will continue to flock to the latest and greatest spiritual experience—until the next one comes along. Just as the house church is quickly becoming popular especially among younger adults, so the expansion of house churches will also come from believers shopping for a new experience. Many of these people will remain involved in house church life only until another novel experience captures their attention.

ANTI-ESTABLISHMENT CHRISTIANS

We do not have to look far in the world of house churches to find individuals who proudly and boldly proclaim that they are "anti-established church" believers. There are numerous websites, articles, and a few books that promote such separatist attitudes from the larger body of Christ in North America. In an attempt to return to a New Testament pattern of healthy united churches, they end up creating more division and problems in the larger body of Christ. The very thing they desire is negated by their attitudes and actions.

Andrew Jones seems to have encountered such a group in his article, "My Gripes about the House Church Movement." He wrote,

> I visited a House Church in the early 90's. . . . A group of disgruntles whose happiness came from the fact they met on Thursday and not Sunday. In a living room and not a sanctuary. On a sofa and not a pew. They were like kids staying away from

school, hiding out, proud of their boldness to leave. And yet in all their freedom they managed only to move the church service from a building to a house. Not much else had changed. Only the location. They had the smirks of naughty boys on their faces. They were a church service on the run. An escaped meeting captured by a living room. One that built its identity from rebellion, defined themselves by what they were not.[9]

Unfortunately, the number of anti-established church believers will continue to increase, and many house churches will grow as a result.

NEW BELIEVERS

The churches represented in this study were selected because they were making disciples. The leaders and members of these churches took seriously our Master's mandate to take the gospel to the fringes of lostness. They are not satisfied with, and many do not desire, transfer growth. Not only do they know the commands of our Lord, but they also go to the fields that are ripe for the harvest. As missional house churches continue to be planted, there will be many that will follow after the pattern of the churches in this study. They will be on mission for Christ in their Jerusalem, Judea and Samaria, and the ends of the earth. May this kind of missiological zeal and practice continue to increase.

CHALLENGES FACING
HOUSE CHURCH LEADERS

While delivering a speech in Paris, Theodore Roosevelt made the following statement:

> It is not the critic who counts, not the man who points out how the strong man stumbled, or where the doer of deeds could have done better. The credit belongs to the man who is actually in the arena, whose face is marred by dust and sweat and blood; who strives valiantly; who errs and comes short again and again, who knows the great enthusiasms, the great devotions, and spends himself in a worthy cause; who at best, knows the triumph of high achievement; and who, at the worst, if he fails, at least fails while daring greatly, so that his place shall never be with those cold and timid souls who know neither victory nor defeat.[10]

The leaders in our study know both victory and defeat. They labor hard. Like all church leaders, they face challenges and frustrations. One leader noted that just because he was a minister with a house church did not mean that the late night phone calls and knocks at his door from those in need of counsel were avoided.

In our study, we asked these church leaders, "What are the greatest challenges you face as a house church leader?" The leaders were not slow to respond, for they have their share of challenges. Here are some of the struggles they face:

- Hostility/apathy from other churches/ministers
- Balancing family/work/ministry
- Low self-worth
- Understanding the Spirit's guidance
- Lack of discipleship in the church
- Lack of unity/community in the church
- Keeping everything simple; valuing relationships over the institution
- Keeping the group from becoming a sect

Of all of the responses received, the three most common challenges were the following:

- Overcoming an inward focus
- Raising up good leaders
- Working with church members who attempt to bring traditional church culture into the house church environment

IRONIC CHALLENGE

It was ironic to hear from these church leaders that one of their major struggles was leading the churches to be outwardly focused. Please remember, these churches were selected for study because they were reaching others with the gospel. The truth learned from these church leaders is that evangelism is challenging work. Even missional churches are quick to become inwardly focused.

Leadership Development

Some time ago, I conducted an informal study of critical issues facing North American church planters. One hundred and ninety participants, representing thirteen denominations, churches, and parachurch organizations, listed leadership development as the second most critical issue.[11] Virtually none of those who participated in this earlier study were involved in house churches. Interestingly, many of the house church leaders represented in this book also noted that raising up leaders was a difficult task. Despite the fact that these churches were reaching people with the gospel and planting other churches, leadership development is a major challenge facing house church leaders.

Traditional Church Culture

We are all part of various cultures. We were born into a particular culture and, unless the Lord returns, we will all die in a particular culture. Culture is not necessarily bad. However, if as an American I go to China and expect the Chinese people to adapt to my culture, I will quickly find myself in problematic situations.

Some of the church leaders expressed frustration with believers who join the house church expecting it to become like a traditional church. Since by their very nature many of these expressions of the body of Christ are more organic and less institutional, more simple and less structured, more relational and less formal, and more participatory and less passive regarding worship and ministry, many of these leaders find themselves ministering to people experiencing significant cultural conflict.

What Can Traditional Churches and House Churches Learn from Each Other?

After discussing in one of my church planting classes our concerns with many North American churches, one student made the accurate summary: "We are sinful people and regardless of the churches of which we are a part, there will always be problems. If we stay in established churches, problems will be present; if we plant new churches, problems will be present." Well said. To his statement, I would add that if the apostle Paul observed problems in the churches he planted, how much more should we expect to experience problems? Remember the old adage? "If you find the perfect church, don't join it or it will become imperfect."

Over the years of my involvement with both very traditional churches and house churches, I have noticed two general concerns: the traditional churches are quick to point out the problems in house churches, and the house churches are quick to point out the problems in traditional churches. Instead of continual infighting among members of the body of Christ, I suggest that we honestly admit our shortcomings, repent of our sins, and be humble enough to learn from one another. Both expressions of church can become steeped in traditionalism, institutionalism, individualism, and pragmatism. Both expressions of church can be evangelistically anemic and inwardly focused. Both expressions of church can be theologically deviant. There is no perfect expression of the body of Christ this side of heaven.

Despite these concerns, much can be learned. For example, many of the traditional churches and denominations have excellent Bible expositors. The teaching ministries of these individuals have much to offer the Church in North America. And house church networks can learn from denominations how to cooperate to accomplish tasks such as missions, benevolence ministries, and biblical (theological) education. On the other hand, traditional churches can learn simplicity, strategies for rapid multiplication, the value of small groups, and biblical and missiological principles of indigenous church planting. House churches have much to contribute regarding healthy expressions of fellowship, high levels of accountability and transparency, and their use of money for missions and ministry.

If the evil one can cause divisions among the body of Christ over local church expressions, then he can hinder the maturation of the North American Church and, thus, the spread of the gospel. May there be no divisions among us over cultural preferences of local church expressions. May the world see our love for one another so that they will know that we are His disciples (John 13:35).

CONCLUSION

Science fiction literature has created worlds in which characters can jump into their time machines and travel to a future time and place to see what life is like. For us, a journey into the future is not possible. The best way to make predictions about the future of house churches is to understand the past and the present.

Rad Zdero, in his book *The Global House Church Movement*, wrote:

> Finally, it has been clear to me that what is going on in North America is a fledgling house church trend.

It is not yet a movement. Those of us immersed in this are certainly at the fringe of the Christian community; it is the road less traveled. It does not seem like much now, but the explosive potential is there. As I survey the immensity of what Jesus is doing globally through the house church movement today, I am gripped by the awesome vision of what the church in North America could become in the years ahead. Sometimes, in communicating vision to people, I like to phrase it this way: "Every Church, Start a Church, Every Year". In the next ten years, this could mean the birth of 1000 house churches in our region. So, for this fellow at least, the future is here![12]

House churches will continue to find a place in North America in the days ahead. It is my prayer that these will be missional house churches and that they will stand firm in sound doctrine and carry out the Great Commission. If the predictions and desires of the leaders in this study foreshadow the future of North American house churches, then over the next ten years North America will experience an exponential increase in the number of such churches. Even in light of the fact that the number of churches will increase, I greatly fear they will not increase through conversion growth, and many house churches will be no different from the many unhealthy traditional churches that are already a part of our religious landscape. If my concern becomes a reality, then the house churches of North America will not be a catalyst for societal transformation through the spreading of the gospel.

Within this book we have studied the house churches that offer the North American Church both encouragement and an example. Though far from perfect, they offer encouragement because they are laboring intentionally in their Jerusalem, Judea, Samaria, and world and are making disciples, baptizing and teaching them to obey all that Christ commanded. These churches offer us an example because, so far, they have been able to remain simple in their approach to being followers of Christ and on mission for Him. They have shown that it is possible to reach people with the gospel and plant churches without all the cultural accoutrements that we in the West believe are necessary for church to exist.

But if, as Zdero wrote, what is currently taking place in North America is a "trend," is there an approaching church planting movement on the horizon? This question will be addressed in the final chapter.

6

Church Planting
Movements and
Missional House Churches

The spontaneous expansion of the Church
reduced to its elements is a very simple thing.
It asks for no elaborate organization, no large
finances, no great numbers of paid missionaries.
In its beginning it may be the work of one man,
and that a man neither learned in the things of
this world, nor rich in the wealth of this world.

—ROLAND ALLEN[1]

*Thus today's paramount task, opportunity,
and imperative in missions is to
multiply churches in the increasing numbers
of receptive peoples of the earth.*

—DONALD A. MCGAVRAN[2]

*Finally, pray for us, brothers, that the Lord's
message may spread rapidly and be honored, just
as it was with you.*

—PAUL, THE APOSTLE[3]

My original intention was not to include this chapter in this book. As I neared the completion of my writing, however, I felt compelled to make this final addition. So what warranted the writing of such a chapter?

The planting of house (or purpose-driven, traditional, cell, postmodern, Reformed, cowboy, etc.) churches is not the answer to reaching North America. We are called to sow the gospel seed and allow the Holy Spirit to work in the hearts of the people to birth churches in their unique cultures. The various cultures of North America will affect the appearance of such churches. The planting of a specific model is not the solution to the problems facing the Church today.

However, over the past fifteen years of both study and involvement in the ministry, I have come to the conviction that, if North America will ever experience church planting movements, they will primarily manifest themselves through simple expressions of the body of Christ with many characteristics of missional house churches. Though such churches may not be true house churches by definition, they will manifest similar characteristics. Though there are serious concerns I have noted throughout this book with the churches in our study in particular and house churches in general, there is much good to be learned from missional house churches.

I recognize that there has been some unpublished discussion surrounding the nature of the churches being planted in the global church planting movements. In some instances, investigators determined that what was being reported as churches was not the case. Sometimes, there were groups of people meeting together, but they were not manifesting the characteristics of New Testament churches. Such discoveries of the truth need to be published. If true churches are not being planted, then we must not count them when reporting church planting movements. I do not desire to see such poor judgment occur in North America. Instead, my desire is to see contextualized biblical churches rapidly multiply across this continent and beyond.

As I have spoken to people from other nations about life in the United States, specifically those living here from non-Western nations, I often hear their desire for the people in their homelands to be able have the great opportunities and freedoms that come with citizenship in the United States of America. Despite the numerous problems we have in this land, people from all over the world desire to know and experience the American Dream. Rightly or wrongly, most North American citizens rarely look to the rest of the world and say, "Wow, I wish we had here what they have there." North Americans by their very nature are self-sufficient and highly individualistic. To desire something from another nation is usually looked on as an unfortunate situation, a display of weakness or dependence, or only a temporary situation until we can provide that commodity by our own ability.

With the North American Church, this attitude is not completely the case. The times are changing. Within the past few decades, reports and stories of church planting movements from across the globe have poured into the offices of mission agencies and churches here in North America. After the initial shock of disbelief regarding amazing church growth rates, and after a season of serious investigation to determine if the reports are true, many have started looking toward the nations in both excitement and anticipation to witness these moves of God.

For the most part, the North American Church is oblivious to church planting movements throughout the world; however, within recent years some attitudes have been changing. Instead of looking at the North American Church and hoping that the world will someday have what we have, many are beginning to desire and pray for the day when North America will experience what is currently taking place over there.

Though there are some groups throughout North America advocating that such movements are occurring within their areas of the continent, as of the time of this writing, I am not aware of the existence of such movements. There may be a general interest in church planting, and there may be many churches involved in this type of missionary work; however, interest and activity alone do not make a church planting movement.

One of the all-time greatest television programs is *The Beverly Hillbillies*.[4] Since I am from Kentucky, you can probably understand why it is a favorite of mine. Every episode consisted of one major theme: communication breakdown. Every episode revealed a group of mountain folk trying to function in one of the most elite environments of the world, Beverly Hills,

California. Viewers were entertained as this backward family interacted with California's finest. Simple objects, words, items, and phrases known to the rest of the United States gained an entirely new meaning when used by the Clampett family, with their limited knowledge of the world beyond their mountain upbringing. A kangaroo became an overgrown rabbit. A swimming pool became a cement pond. They saw Californian culture as unusual because "possum" and "hog back" were nonexistent, delicacies that could only be obtained back home. People who attempted to communicate with the Clampett family always ended up frustrated and misunderstood. Clear communication among the show's characters was impossible.

In this chapter, I hope to avoid a communication breakdown and clear up the confusion many people in North America and beyond have about church planting movements. My experience has been primarily with the North American Church. Therefore, my understanding of church planting movements across the globe has come from those working in international contexts.

My desire is to address questions such as, "What are church planting movements?" "What is the relationship between missional house churches and these movements?" "Where are they supposedly occurring in the world?" "What are the hindrances to such movements?" "What is required for them to occur in North America?" and "Is anything happening on this continent that may be the early signs of approaching church planting movements?"

WHAT ARE CHURCH PLANTING MOVEMENTS?

Long before David Garrison wrote the seminal book, *Church Planting Movements,* Roland Allen, an Anglican missionary to China, wrote his classic, *The Spontaneous Expansion of the Church*. Allen's understanding of church growth has significantly influenced our contemporary understanding of church planting movements. This "spontaneous expansion" to which Allen referred, was summarized in his writing:

> This then is what I mean by spontaneous expansion. I mean the expansion which follows the unexhorted and unorganized activity of individual members of the Church explaining to others the Gospel which they have found for themselves; I mean the expansion which follows the irresistible attraction of the Christian Church for men who see its ordered life, and are drawn to it by desire to discover the secret of a life which they instinctively desire to share; I mean also the expansion of the Church by the addition of new churches.[5]

For Allen, missionaries were to practice the priority of evangelism, work to plant churches and raise up indigenous leadership, and teach the new believers to rely on the Spirit rather than western subsidies and western leaders. In light of these three concepts, Allen staunchly advocated that the missionaries must manifest a "missionary faith." It was this faith that allowed missionaries to commend the churches to the Lord and His word (Acts 20:32) as they continued in the tradition of the apostle Paul, planting other churches. According to Allen, when an indigenous church is empowered by the Holy Spirit and the missionaries who planted that church are manifesting missionary faith, the potential for the spontaneous expansion of the church is very high.[6]

Garrison's widely popular book draws heavily from the

missiology of Allen. According to Garrison, "A Church Planting Movement is *a rapid multiplication of indigenous churches planting churches that sweeps through a people group or population segment.*"[7] Let's consider the words in this definition.

RAPID

In a successful church planting movement, the speed at which people come to faith in Christ and churches are birthed is very quick. In some movements, many missionaries have a difficult time keeping track of the numbers of new believers and new churches. New believers commonly lead others to the faith, and newly planted churches plant other churches. The conversion growth rate that occurs always outstrips the population growth of the area.

MULTIPLICATION

Rather than church planting by addition (where a congregation plants another church here and there, and maybe those new churches will eventually plant other churches), it is reported that in church planting movements, the number of new churches increases exponentially. Two churches become four churches, and then the four become eight, and so on. In church planting movements, it is normal for all churches, regardless of their age or financial resources, to be involved in church planting.

INDIGENOUS

The churches being planted in such movements are springing from the cultural context and thereby look and feel culturally appropriate for the environment. Also, though missionaries may be significantly involved in planting the first churches when the movement begins, the indigenous people, not the outsiders, are the ones taking the lead in planting the other churches.

CHURCHES PLANTING CHURCHES

Missionaries may plant the first few churches in a particular area; however, there comes a time when the indigenous churches themselves begin to plant churches. At some point, a critical mass is reached and a tipping point occurs, starting a chain reaction of churches that plant churches that plant churches.

PEOPLE GROUP OR POPULATION SEGMENT

In the early days of church planting movements, communicating the gospel usually occurs among a particular ethnolinguistic or affinity group. Within this group, there are natural relationships whereby the gospel travels freely from acquaintance to acquaintance and from family member to family member. Though these movements usually begin in a homogenous unit, soon the gospel spreads beyond the same people and among those of different ethnicities, races, and classes.

WHAT IS THE RELATIONSHIP BETWEEN MISSIONAL HOUSE CHURCHES AND THESE MOVEMENTS?

Garrison noted that, in the research that has been conducted on global church planting movements, house churches are found in every movement. Though he did not use the term *missional*, many characteristics of the churches he described are similar to those of the missional house churches in my research.

Please understand that I am not advocating that house

churches are the missing link in the chain for North American church planting movements. They are not a panacea to our problems. The presence of house churches, however, does help establish an environment and support principles conducive to church planting movements.

Some time ago, I watched the men's speed skating competition in the Winter Olympics. I was amazed at the sleekness of their uniforms. There was no loose fabric so wind resistance would be kept to a minimum. As the competitors rounded the track, they leaned forward, again to reduce resistance. These men truly believed that they could hinder their chances at winning a gold medal if they wore improper clothing and if they failed to maintain the proper posture. No skater would enter the competition wearing jeans and a Hawaiian shirt or fail to lean into the curves.[8]

Though there are many cultural accoutrements that a church can embrace that will not necessarily disqualify it from being a New Testament church, those same preferences can hinder church planting movements. Just as Olympic skaters attempt to eliminate anything that would create resistance, likewise, this expression of church assists in eliminating many of the barriers to the movements. For example, Garrison notes the following strengths of house churches:

- Leadership responsibilities remain small and manageable.
- If heresies do occur, they are confined by the small size of the house church. Like a leak that appears in the hull of a great ship, the heresy can be sealed off in a single compartment without endangering the whole.

- You can't hide in a small group, so accountability is amplified.
- Member care is easier, because everyone knows everyone.
- Because house church structure is simple, it is easier to reproduce.
- Small groups tend to be much more efficient at evangelism and assimilation of new believers.
- Meeting in homes positions the church closer to the lost.
- House churches blend into the community, rendering them less visible to persecutors.
- Basing in the home keeps the church's attention on daily life issues.
- The very nature of rapidly multiplying house churches promotes the rapid development of new church leaders.[9]

WHERE ARE THEY OCCURRING IN THE WORLD?

Garrison devoted several chapters of his book to discussing the various locations where church planting movements are supposedly occurring. I do not know how many of these movements have been confirmed by additional researchers. A large section of Garrison's work advocates that movements have occurred in Africa, the Muslim world, Latin America, and Europe. Though he also addressed movements in various parts of the Asian world, he spent significant time discussing where the largest movements have been occurring—India and China. The reader is literally taken on a globetrotting expedition. The following statements and various case studies pepper this book:

- In Madhya Pradesh State, a Church Planting Movement produced 4,000 new churches in less than seven years.
- In the 1990s nearly 1,000 new churches were planted in Orissa with another 1,000 new outreach points. By 2001 a new church was being started every 24 hours.
- In China more than 30,000 believers are baptized every day.
- A Church Planting Movement in a northern Chinese province sees 20,000 new believers and 500 new churches started in less than a five year period.
- Despite government attempts to eliminate Christianity, a Church Planting Movement in one Southeast Asian country adds more than 50,000 new believers in one five year period.
- During the decade of the nineties, Church Planting Movements in Outer Mongolia and Inner Mongolia produced more than 60,000 new believers.
- In eight months, 28 Ethiopian evangelists led 681 persons to Christ and started 83 new churches.
- Each month an estimated 1,200 new churches are started in Africa.
- More Muslims have come to Christ in the past two decades than at any other time in history.

- In North Africa, more than 16,000 Berbers turned to Christ over a two-decade period.
- In an Asian Muslim country, more than 150,000 Muslims embrace Jesus and gather in more than 3,000 locally led Isa Jamaats (Jesus Groups).
- During the decade of the 1990s, Christians in a Latin American country overcame relentless government persecution to grow from 235 churches to more than 4,000 churches, with 40,000 converts awaiting baptism.
- Church Planting Movement practitioners report in 1999, among the refugees of the Netherlands, 45 new churches were started in a single year.

What Are the Hindrances to Such Movements?

As a child, I remember my mother having to clean the gutters on our house every year. Our property was next to a wooded area. As the leaves on the trees started to fall in autumn, the wind naturally blew some of those leaves onto our roof and into our gutters. When the rains would come, the gutters overflowed due to the obstacles that had collected there.

In a similar fashion, we need to be aware of the obstacles to church planting movements and make certain that those obstacles are removed from future missionary practice. In the booklet *Church Planting Movements*, which preceded Garrison's book by the same title, he delineated nine specific obstacles to these movements. The following discussion is taken from his original booklet.[10]

IMPOSING EXTRA-BIBLICAL REQUIREMENTS FOR BEING A CHURCH

Though much has already been said about this issue, Garrison noted that this problem is also an issue outside of North America when missionaries are quick to bring their cultural expectations rather than the teachings of Christ to new churches. Some of their expectations become obstacles in the pathways of the churches.

LOSS OF VALUED CULTURAL IDENTITY

When missionaries import their cultures from their homeland into the new churches, movement is hindered. People quickly come to believe that being a follower of Christ requires becoming North American or European. Unfortunately, this trend has been going on for years. Much of colonialism was defined by this approach to missions. People were required to lose their cultural identities and embrace those of the missionaries. The impact of this problem is seen whenever someone gathers with a church on Sunday morning in Africa, only to realize that the church's meeting place, order of worship, music, and preaching style are practically the same as those found in Smalltown, U.S.A.

OVERCOMING BAD EXAMPLES OF CHRISTIANITY

In areas of the world where believers have set a poor example of what it means to follow Christ, many unbelievers recognize the hypocrisy and have no desire for such a faith. I recall prayer-walking the streets of St. John's, Newfoundland, and seeing the impact of this barrier firsthand. As I shared the gospel with many young adults, I was quickly told, "I don't want anything to do with Christianity. I've experienced the corruption in the Catholic Church (or, it was the Anglican Church if I was speaking to a Protestant), and Christianity is all about bondage and restricting people."

On the other hand, in areas of the world where local churches are not actively involved in intentionally sharing the gospel (which is also considered a bad example), obviously, the likelihood for any movement to occur is practically nonexistent.

NONREPRODUCIBLE CHURCH MODELS

Whenever missionaries use methods for evangelism, teaching, and leadership development that cannot be reproduced by the new churches, then the possibility for movement is hindered. Several times in his writings, the apostle Paul reminded the churches to imitate him, which of course required a doctrinal commitment and a lifestyle that could be reproduced. For example, to the Corinthian church, he wrote, "Therefore I urge you, be imitators of me. This is why I have sent to you Timothy, who is my beloved and faithful child in the Lord. He will remind you about my ways in Christ Jesus, just as I teach everywhere in every church" (1 Corinthians 4:16–17).

Though by western standards the missionary's paradigms may be more efficient and of a higher caliber, they may not necessarily be the best approach to facilitate church planting movements.

SUBSIDIES CREATING DEPENDENCY

Though money is not necessarily a problem, it can be an obstacle to movement. North Americans are compassionate people, and we are quick to send money to meet global needs.

In areas of the world where North American financial subsidies have been sent and have (intentionally or unintentionally) created a welfare mentality among the people, the likelihood of those churches ever believing that they can do anything without North American dollars is slim. Garrison noted, "When well-intentioned outsiders prop up growth by purchasing buildings or subsidizing pastors' salaries, they limit the capacity of the movement to reproduce itself spontaneously and indigenously."[11] In the process of teaching people how to be the church, we must allow them to do so in their own cultural expressions and with their own financial means.

EXTRA-BIBLICAL LEADERSHIP REQUIREMENTS

The potential for church planting movements decreases whenever the requirements for church leadership exceed the New Testament prescriptions. Clearly, outstanding moral, theological, ethical, and familial standards carry more weight (for example, 1 Timothy 3; Titus 1) than many Western cultural expectations such as sophisticated leadership training, college and graduate degrees, and a full-time salary. There is nothing inherently wrong with these cultural preferences. Many times, healthy contextualization demands them. However, we must always remember that the biblical prescriptions alone are sufficient.

LINEAR, SEQUENTIAL THOUGHT AND PRACTICE

In most western contexts we usually think in linear and sequential terms. We tend to advocate practices that are derived from a step-by-step philosophy (that is, first, second, third). Many missionaries who have been involved in church planting movements are careful to not follow such patterns. For example, in the West we naturally think that someone entering into a new culture should first learn the language, second start sharing the gospel, and third plant churches. Instead, many are suggesting that missionaries begin sharing the gospel before learning the language. It has also been shown that even before people come to faith in Christ, they are already participating in church-related gatherings. There is no set formula for producing a church planting movement. Many movements occur when the various components of such movements occur simultaneously.

Planting "Frog" Rather Than "Lizard" Churches

Garrison used metaphors to describe two different types of churches. The "frog" churches, like a frog that sits and waits for food to come to it, are churches that expect unbelievers to come to them. On the other hand, Garrison advocated planting "lizard" churches. These churches, like a lizard that scurries everywhere looking for food, are those congregations that are actively involved in their communities and constantly reaching out to unbelievers.

Prescriptive Strategies

Missionaries who enter into areas with highly complex, preconceived church planting strategies, sometimes create barriers to church planting movements. Instead missionaries should prayerfully study their contexts and see where God is working among the people. Instead of coming to the field with all the answers, missionaries must come as learners and allow their church planting strategies to develop from within the context in which they minister.

What Is Required for Church Planting Movements to Occur in North America?

Apart from the sovereignty of God, church planting movements will not occur anywhere in North America or anywhere in the world. Jesus informed Nicodemus, "The wind blows where it pleases, and you hear its sound, but you don't know where it comes from or where it is going. So it is with everyone born of the Spirit."[12] God Himself speaking through the prophet Isaiah was clear, "For My thoughts are not your thoughts, and your ways are not My ways."[13] The message of the Scriptures is that God will accomplish His plans whether or not you and I are involved in the process. I believe God does desire to use the North American Church to spread His glory both outside and on this continent. I do not believe He is finished with North America and has now moved on to another part of the world.

The question that we must ask ourselves is, "If God desires to pour out His Spirit on North America, what can we do to join Him in His work, rather than hinder the work?" God desired His children to enter into the Promised Land, and enter they did, but forty years after the original entrance date and after the death of many. My desire is that we who live in North America will not find ourselves wandering for forty years and miss the possible blessings of God.

From a humanistic perspective, what are the necessary shifts that are required before North America will experience church planting movements? In other words, as a follower of Christ, what are the things for which I am responsible in the facilitation of such movements? Though we cannot manipulate God's sovereignty or control the contextual environment of North America, we do have ability to make personal and institutional adjustments in light of what is common among church planting movements.

An Ecclesiological Shift

One significant adjustment that is necessary for the North American Church to make, albeit the most difficult, concerns understanding the local church. *The most critical issue in North American church planting today is an ecclesiological issue.* We have a difficult time accepting the idea that local churches can be true New Testament congregations, manifesting all of the distinctions of a healthy church, apart from many of our cultural accoutrements. For example, buildings, money, well-organized programs, and highly skilled musicians are not necessary for a church to exist. Though, in many cases, they are wonderful blessings to have, they can be a hindrance to a healthy understanding of church. As long as the North American Church believes that many of our cultural expectations for church are required, church planting movements will probably be a future impossibility.

An examination of Church history reveals the sociological reality that over time groups and organizations of people move from the simple to the complex. What begins as something low in structure and organization eventually becomes higher in structure and organization and difficult to reproduce. German theologian and Church historian Adolph Harnack once wrote of how Christianity spread across the globe so rapidly within a few hundred years. Though he wrote these words over a hundred years ago, they are a challenge to us today.

> *This* religion was the first to cut the ground from under the feet of all other religions, and by means of her religious philosophy, as a civilizing power, to

displace ancient philosophy. But the reasons for the triumph of Christianity in that age are no guarantee for the permanence of that triumph throughout the history of mankind. Such a triumph rather depends upon the simple elements of the religion, on the preaching of the living God as the Father of men, and on the likeness of Jesus Christ. For that very reason it depends also on the capacity of Christianity to strip off once more any collective syncretism and unite itself to fresh coefficients.[14]

Continually returning to Scriptures to properly understand the local church is a necessity, albeit a painful one at times. By no means am I suggesting that traditional, well-established churches have to drop all of their traditions and discard their cultures. This would obviously cause more harm than good to the body of Christ. Neither am I stating that traditional churches will have no effective future ministries in North America. Many will play a key role in sending, supporting, and nurturing church planting teams that will serve as catalysts for church planting movements. Also, many traditional churches will continue to experience growth and will continue to have a significant impact on societal transformation in their communities. Let me be absolutely clear: the traditional church in North America is not dead and is extremely valuable to the future of North American church planting.

My words in this chapter are primarily to those who will be planting churches. Make certain you sow the gospel seed in the hearts of people. Work to keep from importing your cultural desires onto them, if those structures will hinder their growth in Christ and keep them from effectively spreading the gospel and planting churches. No missionary can be culturally neutral. We can, however, be cautious with our cultural preferences.

A Strategic Shift

The second major shift necessary prepare for North American church planting movements is a strategic shift. Many church planting strategies being advocated by prominent church planters and pastors lack a philosophy that embraces church multiplication; they advocate church planting by addition, at best. This philosophy can also be seen in much of the church planting literature and conferences throughout North America.

Church planters need to advocate strategies that model the philosophy of reproduction at a variety of levels. Highly technical strategies usually hinder church planting movements since they are difficult to reproduce by ordinary Christians. Church planters need to understand that they model before believers not only the Christian life but also how to plant churches. We reproduce what we know; we know what has been modeled before us. When others see church planters develop technical strategies, technical church structures and organizations, and use a technical form of leadership, then the potential for church multiplication is very low.

Church planting strategies need to be developed emphasize planting simple expressions of churches that are highly reproducible by any God-called believer. If all church planting strategies require technical knowledge of missiology and theology, and can be carried out only by those who are professional church planters, then the majority of our converts will be educated in a form of church planting that most will never be able to imitate, even if God calls them to plant churches.

At the time of this writing, Rachel, my youngest daughter

(one-and-a-half years old), is already starting to imitate Hannah, her older sister (three years old). She wants to participate in the activities in which Hannah is involved. She wants to mimic the motions of her older sister. Church planting strategies need to be developed with the understanding that just as a child learns by observation, likewise our children in the faith learn from us by observation.

Church planting strategies need to reflect the priority of evangelism. One of my concerns with church planting in North America is that much of what is taking place is based on the transfer of believers from other churches into the new churches. We must remember that, throughout the world where church planting movements are occurring, abundant evangelism is taking place. Throughout the New Testament, we observe that the Church grew through conversion growth. The apostles made disciples (evangelized) and then gathered them into churches.

Church planting strategies need to embrace the principle of "phase-out." Tom Steffen popularized this concept in his book *Passing the Baton*.[15] The apostle Paul modeled the basic ideal behind phase-out. When Paul entered a city and evangelized some of the people, he gathered the believers into congregations and appointed elders over the churches. Later, the apostle moved on to repeat the process. Of the churches he planted, he never became permanently attached to any congregation as their pastor. He removed himself from the areas with the expectation that the new churches would continue making disciples. He would later visit, write, or send others back to minister to the new churches while he moved on to plant other churches.

Throughout the non-Western world, many missionaries who participate in church planting movements are not planting churches and pastoring those churches. Instead, they plant churches, raise up pastoral leaders, and move on to repeat the process. Though there is nothing wrong with a few missionaries planting churches and remaining permanently fixed to those churches, we must understand that church planting movements are occurring where the majority of the missionaries are releasing the new, Spirit-filled believers to be the church in their areas with their own leaders. Most importantly, we must remember that the weight of the New Testament model for church planters is that those missionaries do not remain permanent fixtures.

A Methodological Shift

A third shift that needs to occur to prepare the North American Church for church planting movements is a change in our methods. Church planters must understand that all church planting methods are not appropriate for all cultures and are not always conducive for church planting movements. Just because a particular church planting approach worked well in one area of the United States does not necessarily mean that the same method will work well in another context. Church planting movements will take place where churches are being planted with a variety of highly contextualized and highly reproducible methods, instead of a single one-size-fits-all approach.

There are many methods regarding the how-to of church planting; however, we must remember that some methods are more likely to result in church multiplication than other methods. Our church planting methods must be evaluated in light of three questions. First, do the church planting methods accurately communicate the death, burial, and resurrection of Christ and the basic essence and function of the church to the new believers; or, are the church planting methods adding significant North American cultural expectations to what it means to follow

Christ and to be the church? Second, are the church planting methods effective in making disciples and raising up leaders for the harvest; or, are the church planting methods causing the new believers to depend on the church planters for their teaching, evangelism, leadership, financial support, decision-making, and worship expressions? Third, are the church planting methods simple and easily reproduced by ordinary Christians; or, do they require years of training and develop highly technical skills before they can be contextually applied?

WHAT IS GOING ON IN NORTH AMERICA?

In 2000 Garrison published a booklet entitled *Church Planting Movements* that was an early attempt to define, identify, and describe such movements.[16] After reading the booklet, I was discouraged to see no mention of church planting movements in North America. My discouragement stemmed not from Garrison overlooking this continent but rather from a reality that a true movement was not occurring here.

One of the first things I noticed about Garrison's 2004 book, *Church Planting Movements*, was that he devoted a chapter to what is happening in North America. I wondered if Garrison had uncovered something that reflects what is taking place throughout the world. I was skeptical. But what did this chapter on North America have to do with church planting movements?

CHAPTER TEN—"NORTH AMERICA"

If such movements ever occur here in a Western, postindustrialized, postmodern, and post-Christianized land, they will not look like those found in many Eastern nations. Here people are highly individualized and consumer-oriented regarding faith issues. Here the family ties and extensive social networks of kith and kin are miniscule compared to the peoples of other nations currently experiencing these movements. If church planting movements occur within the current sociological milieu of North America, the greatest growth will probably occur among affinity lines, rather than familial lines of individuals who are fairly postmodern in their thinking and/or quite possibly marginalized in regard to power and wealth.

In many nations that have little or no access to the gospel, there are few poor examples of Christianity to overcome. In North America there are numerous poor examples that influence our society. Also, in nations where the nuclear family, as well as the extended family, is highly connected, the gospel can spread faster and new churches can be stronger than in nations where the family unit has disintegrated. If church planting movements occur in North America, as it stands today, the resulting church growth will be slower than the growth rate of other nations.

Garrison's chapter addressing North America seems to be out of place in regard to the rest of the book. Rather than being a description of contemporary movements taking place in North America, he threw the reader a slight curve. Chapter 10 is really a challenge to the North American Church in light of what God is doing throughout the world *and what He has done historically in America.* Garrison did offer some contemporary examples of possible precursors to church planting movements, but no movements are described.

Referencing Kenneth Scott Latourette, Garrison opened this chapter with the following: "Of all the great advances that Christianity made during this period [nineteenth century], none was more significant than the discipling and congregationalizing of North America."[17] For the next several pages, he discussed the pioneer advancement as well as evangelism and church planting along the frontier settlements. He noted that, by the end of the nineteenth century, almost every North American town had some Protestant community.

Garrison then raised some questions: "How did this pioneering movement spread the gospel with such determination from the Atlantic to the Pacific shore? Twenty-first century denominations look back to their pioneer forefathers and struggle to understand the kind of zeal that subdued an untamed continent. Images of circuit riding preachers, brush arbor revivals, and Great Awakenings propelled the movement across the territory, but what kinds of churches were able to keep pace with this rapid expansion?"[18]

Garrison's case study here is the archetypal frontier church, Sandy Creek Baptist Church, planted in rural North Carolina in 1755. In seventeen years, this congregation became a mother, grandmother, and great grandmother to forty-two churches from which 125 ministers emerged.

Citing historian Robert Baker, Garrison noted that "within three years of the Separates' settlement at Sandy Creek there were three fully constituted churches with a combined membership of over nine hundred."[19] Noting that Elliott Smith cited William Cathcart writing in 1881, Garrison included, "There are today probably thousands of churches that arose from the efforts of Shubal Sterrns and the churches of Sandy Creek."[20]

Before discussing the contemporary North American context, he concluded his historical reflection with a challenging summarization:

> Passion, evangelism, biblicism, local church autonomy, uneducated lay leaders, missionary zeal,

rapid multiplication of converts, and new churches, fearless advance through persecution—all these were characteristics of the Sandy Creek tradition.

Viewed through the lens of modern day Church Planting Movements, it is easy to add the Sandy Creek tradition to the list. By today's standards, Sandy Creek seems exceptional, but it was only one of a number of frontier churches that won the North American continent in the 18th and 19th centuries. Those that lacked Sandy Creek's explosive DNA simply did not flourish or even survive.

If this was the legacy of the 19th century American Protestantism, then where does that tradition stand today?[21]

Following a brief discussion of the number of Christian adherents in North America and a brief reference to mega-churches, Garrison noted that cultural shifts and population growth have attributed to a decline in the once-prominent role of the Church in Western society. Despite the grim reality of the rapidly diminishing influence of the Church, Garrison offered his readers some hope for a "Sandy Creek renaissance" and that "a surprising number of Christian leaders are adopting a radical new vision that looks surprisingly like other movements that we've witnessed around the world."[22]

For the next several pages, he briefly mentioned the ministries and sometimes the missiologies of certain individuals and groups. The first of those listed are examples of house church planters. Some of those referenced are Dan Mahew of the Summit House Church Network in Portland; a few house churches in Canada; Jonathan and Jennifer Campbell's work with a network of house churches in California (Riverside, Los Angeles, Pasadena, Santa

Cruz, San Diego, San Jose, San Francisco), Orlando, Boise, and in Seattle and Kitsap County, Washington; and Neil and Dana Cole with Church Multiplication Associates, a ministry that encompasses nine house church networks located in seven states and two countries. In 2001 Church Multiplication Associates averaged one church plant each week.

The second listing of contemporary examples is related to cell churches and those churches that have witnessed significant growth through home fellowship groups. Larry Kreider of DOVE Christian Fellowship, Rick Warren of Saddleback Valley Community Church, Bill Hybels of Willow Creek Community Church, and Larry Stockstill of Bethany World Prayer Center are mentioned.

Garrison also noted that groups such as the Chicago Metro Baptist Association and the Union Baptist Association of greater Houston have adopted visions for church planting movements within their regions. The Dallas Baptist Association appointed Joseph Cartwright to serve as a house church planter. Garrison concluded his examples with the North American Mission Board of the Southern Baptist Convention as embracing the vision of a "New Testament church planting movement among all people groups in the United States, U.S. territories, and Canada."[23]

He ended this chapter offering a strong challenge to his readers: "Can Church Planting Movements emerge in 21st century North America? Have North American evangelicals lost their Sandy Creek legacy to the comforts of the institutional church with its professional clergy, air-conditioned nurseries, and graded choir programs? Has America, like Esau, traded its Sandy Creek birthright for a bowl of pottage? North America may yet have another Sandy Creek era ahead of it. These are yeasty times."[24]

What Is in the Book for Us?

It seems that Garrison wrote chapter 10 to fulfill a three-fold purpose. First, by encouraging his North American readers to remember their history, he explained that such movements are not a foreign concept to this continent. In the past, God has blessed us with rapid and multiplicative growth of indigenous churches.

Second, though he documented no contemporary examples of North American movements, by reminding us that the vision for these movements is already found among many people, he leads his readers to believe that North America may be in the very early stages of preparation for church planting movements.

Several times throughout his book, Garrison noted the importance of house church planting. His penchant is definitely for such expressions of the Church. By offering evidence of those who are strategizing to plant missional house churches, Garrison made the point that some North Americans have embraced this paradigm. He referenced those who have seen thousands come to Christ through cell churches and home-based small groups to praise their work and to note that these models of church life were not leading to church planting movements in other parts of the world. When discussing the difference between cell churches and house churches, he wrote, "While cell churches enjoy many of the initial qualities of Church Planting Movements, they tend to reach a plateau owing to the internal controls associated with centralized leadership."[25]

Garrison's third purpose for writing is to challenge the North American Church to consider revising its ecclesiology and missiology. Though Garrison never stated that this is the challenge of his chapter, the contemporary North American believer cannot help but be faced with the reality of examining his or her church's health and growth in comparison to the early frontier churches.

The reader is challenged to reflect on a time when believers on this continent held to a very simple, yet biblical understanding of church that was easily translated from context to context through passionate evangelists and to understand that some believers are returning to very similar understandings today.

This challenge causes us to ponder the basics necessary for churches to exist. We are confronted with the irony that though we make up the wealthiest, most educated, and most trained Church in the world, the North American Church in general is not growing. Are many of the cultural church necessities biblically necessary for a church to exist and grow? Have we bowed to the gods of North American consumerism, professionalism, individualism, pragmatism, and traditionalism, thus substituting a biblical ecclesiology for a culturally palatable one? These and other inevitable questions naturally come to mind as one reads Garrison's chapter 10.

CONCLUSION

A story was once told about a wise old man who was highly revered by the people in his village. People from near and far went to the sage, seeking his wisdom prior to making major decisions. His reputation was impeccable and his discernment was fascinating. One day a group of irreverent boys developed a ploy to prove the man a fool and cause him to lose face before the villagers. They captured a young sparrow and showed it to the old man while inquiring if he believed the bird was alive or dead. "If the man says, 'The bird is alive,'" they discussed, "then the one holding the bird will use his thumb to break the bird's neck and then hold the dead bird in the air for all to see. However, if the sage states that the bird is dead, then the one of us holding the bird will simply release the bird into the air proving the man wrong."

The next day when many people were in the marketplace and the old man was passing through, the boys quickly gathered and hailed the man. "Tell me, sir," the leader of the gang inquired, "this bird that I'm holding, is it dead or alive?" By this time, several villagers had gathered around listening with great anticipation for his answer. Recognizing that the troublesome youth had concocted a ruse to bring shame to him, the old man stared silently at the group for what seemed to be an eternity. After the silence had created an atmosphere so thick with tension that its weight was suffocating, the young man exclaimed angrily, "Tell me, old man, is the bird dead or alive?"

While acknowledging his opponent with a subtle grin, the old sage simply responded, "My son, the answer is in your hand."

It is my hope and prayer that if the sovereign Lord so desires to move across the North American continent, blessing his Church with church planting movements, you and I are participants rather than observers (or worse, hindrances) of such activities. Though we cannot create church planting movements, we can establish obstacles to such movements. And, in such a case, the answer to us personally experiencing such movements is in our hands.

Garrison concluded his book with encouraging words:

> *It can't happen here.* This is what they said in Vietnam until they saw it in Cambodia. It's what they said in Cambodia before they saw it in China. It's what they said it Central America before they saw it in

Bogotá. It's what they said in Sudan before they saw it in Ethiopia. Perhaps it's what they are saying where you live.[26]

What are "they" saying where you live? More importantly, what are you saying *and doing*?

Appendix 1

Research Methodology

This book is based on an informal research project I conducted in the fall of 2004. Since I had neither a budget nor a paid research team, I realized that the project would be very simple in nature. I began this task wanting to know, "Where are the North American house churches that are experiencing both baptisms and the planting of other churches?" A secondary question was, "What are the various characteristics of such churches and their leaders?"

A research project of this nature required two phases. Phase I was an initial web-based survey (see appendix 2) that allowed me to determine which churches were experiencing both baptisms and church planting. Phase II consisted of one-hour telephone interviews with the church leaders who participated in Phase I, revealing characteristics of their churches.

With these questions in mind and the survey tool developed, I contacted everyone I knew who could put me in touch with house church leaders who could participate in my study. Tony Dale with *House2House* magazine graciously offered to send out an e-mail to his readers along with the link to my web-based survey. This process generated 297 responses from around the world. With help from Neil Cole, another seventeen participants took the web-based survey, making the total participants 314. After eliminating the non-North American participants, I was left with 255 participants.

After Phase I, I counted the churches that had experienced at least one baptism in the previous year and had planted at least one church in the past three years. After applying these two screens, I was left with ninety-one eligible churches.

Phase II began when I, along with Sam Dyer and Dan Rice, both students at The Southern Baptist Theological Seminary, began contacting these ninety-one church leaders for a lengthy phone survey (see appendix 3). Some of the church-growth research questionnaires developed by Thom S. Rainer served as a model for my Phase II phone survey. Of the ninety-one eligible participants, we were able to contact and interview thirty-three. All of the participants in this study were promised confidentiality.

I then coded the data and entered it into a spreadsheet for usability.

REFLECTIONS ON THE RESEARCH METHODOLOGY

It should be noted that this was not a highly standardized research project. My sample was not selected by usual procedures that allowed me to draw randomly from a pool of all the house churches in North America. Snowball sampling would best describe my approach to locating survey participants. Because house churches and their leaders tend to be "hidden" from researchers, it is obviously difficult to locate them. I began working through my acquaintances to identify participants. Because snowball sampling is subject to numerous biases, I tried not to generalize from the churches studied in this book to the larger North American house church population. Though this sampling procedure at times makes it difficult to generalize, this was not a major challenge to this research project. My work here was both exploratory and descriptive rather than an attempt to explain fully North American house churches or the House Church Movement. This study has profiled a subcategory of the North American house church, the missional house church.

FUTURE RESEARCH

At the time of this writing, this research project is the first of its kind on the North American house church. I am unaware of any extensive research being conducted on house churches in general or missional house churches in particular. Because of the great dearth of information, it is my hope that the strengths and limitations of my work in this book will challenge and motivate others to conduct better future studies.

Appendix 2

_____

Phase I
Web-based Questionnaire

CHURCH SURVEY
NOVEMBER 2004

In order to better understand house churches, we are conducting the following survey. Please complete, as accurately as possible, the following questions.

In what country is your church located?

_____

In what state or province is your church located?

_____

In the past year, how many people has your church baptized?

- o   0
- o   1–3
- o   4–6
- o   7–9
- o   10+

On average, within the past three years, how many people did your church baptize each year?

- o   Not Applicable—we are not three years old
- o   0
- o   1–3
- o   4–6
- o   7–9
- o   10+

If your church has experienced baptisms within the past year, what means/methods did you use to reach those people from the harvest?

_____

_____

In the past three years, how many churches has your church planted (started)?

- o   0
- o   1–3
- o   4–6
- o   7–9
- o   10+

What are the greatest challenges you face as a house church leader?

_____

_____

May we contact you to speak further regarding your responses to the previous questions?

Yes (please provide your contact information below)

No

CONTACT INFORMATION

Please provide your contact information in the appropriate fields:

Name:

Phone:

E-Mail:

THANK YOU FOR PARTICIPATING IN
THE SURVEY PROCESS.

Phase II

Phone Survey Questionnaire for North American Churches with Both Baptisms and Church Plants

Name of Respondent:

Respondent Number:

Phone:

E-mail:

Date:

GEOGRAPHICAL QUESTIONS

1) Your Location (city, state/province)

2) Does the church meet in this location?

3) Which area best describes the location in which your church meets:

a) Open country/rural area
b) Town (500–2,499 population)
c) Small city (2,500–9,999 population)
d) Medium city/downtown (10,000–49,999 population)
e) Medium city/suburbs (10,000–49,999 population)
f) Large city/downtown or inner city (50,000+ population)
g) Large city/suburbs (50,000+ population)

Church Questions

4) How many years have you been meeting together as a house church?

_____ Less than 1
_____ 1–3
_____ 4–6
_____ 7–9
_____ 10–12
_____ 13 or more

5) Does your individual house church gather weekly for worship and fellowship?

YES / NO

6) When your individual house church gathers for worship and fellowship, do you usually meet in a house?

YES / NO

6a) If not, please list the physical structure or location of the meeting.

7) Is your church a part of a network of house churches?

YES / NO

7a) If yes, please give name of network.

7b) How many churches are in that network (if known)?

7c) Do all of the churches within your network ever meet together as a whole for worship/fellowship?

YES / NO

> 7c1) If yes, how often?
>
> 7c2) If yes, please list the location(s) of the network meeting (e.g., house).

7d) Do elders oversee the network of churches?

YES /NO

> 7d1) If yes, what are their primary responsibilities?
>
> 7d2) If yes, do these elders receive regular financial support from the network of churches?
>
> YES / NO

8) Is your individual house church a part of a denomination?

YES / NO

8a) If yes, please give name of denomination.

9) When your individual house church gathers for worship and fellowship, what is usually the size of the church present?

_____ 2–5

_____ 6–9

_____ 10–13

_____ 14–17

_____ 18–21

_____ 22–25

_____ 26–29

_____ 30–33

_____ 34+

10) Are pastors/elders a part of your individual house church's leadership?

> YES / NO

>> 10a) If yes, do these pastors/elders receive regular financial support from the house church?
>> YES / NO

11) Are deacons a part of your individual house church's leadership?

> YES / NO

12) Please define evangelism as your church understands the term:

13) Please describe in some detail what your church believes must take place for a person to be "born again."

14) How does your church know when a believer has a "sense of belonging and is thus involved in the life and ministry of the church?"

15) Are there any requirements/expectations (ex. new members' class, covenant) for being a "member" of your house church?

> YES / NO

>> 15a) If yes, please list them.

16) Does your individual church regularly collect financial tithes/offerings?

> YES / NO

>> 16a) If yes, what are some of the general uses of these tithes/offerings?

CHURCH DEMOGRAPHICS

17) Race

What percentage of your individual house church is:

Caucasian   _____%
African-American _____%
Hispanic   _____%
Asian   _____%
Other_____ _____%
    Total 100%

18) Age

What percentage of your individual house church is:

Under 18   _____%
19–35   _____%
36–50   _____%
51–66   _____%
66+   _____%
    Total 100%

19) Economic Levels

Of the new believers whom your individual house church has recently seen come to faith in Christ, financially speaking, what percentage are:

Upper class   _____%
Middle class   _____%
Lower class   _____%
    Total 100%

Personal Leadership Questions

20) As a house church leader, how are you raising up leaders in your church (steps involved, processes, resources used, etc.)?

21) Please respond accordingly to the following statement: "My approach to leadership development is working well."
   1) Strongly Agree
   2) Agree
   3) Uncertain
   4) Disagree
   5) Strongly Disagree

22) What are your primary responsibilities as a house church leader?

23) Please share your highest level of education attained.
   1) Less than High School
   2) High School
   3) Some College
   4) College Degree
   5) Some graduate school
   6) Graduate Degree
   7) Some Doctoral Studies
   8) Doctoral Degree
      23a) If respondent has completed graduate studies, ask if they have attended a seminary? If they have, please get the name of the institution.

24) Please respond to the following statement:

"The Bible is the Word of God without any error."
   1) Strongly Agree
   2) Agree
   3) Unsure
   4) Disagree
   5) Strongly Disagree

25) What/who has been the most helpful resource or person to you as a house church leader?

26) In general, what do you think will become of house churches in North America in the next 10 years?

MISCELLANEOUS QUESTIONS

27) Is there any information that you believe would be helpful to others through our study, which we have not already asked you about?
   YES / NO
      27a) If yes, list comments.

28) If we need additional information, may we contact you again the future?
   YES / NO

Thank you for participating in our study of North American house churches.

Appendix 4

Common Characteristics of Every Church Planting Movement[1]

- Extraordinary prayer
- Abundant evangelism
- Intentional planting of reproducing churches
- The authority of God's Word
- Local leadership
- Lay leadership
- House churches
- Churches planting churches
- Rapid reproduction
- Healthy churches

Appendix 5

Characteristics of Most Church Planting Movements[1]

- A climate of uncertainty in society
- Insulation from outsiders
- A high cost for following Christ
- Bold fearless faith
- Family-based conversion patterns
- Rapid incorporation of new believers
- Worship in the heart language
- Divine signs and wonders
- On-the-job leadership training
- Missionaries suffered

Notes

Introduction

1. For example, Philip and Phoebe Anderson, *The House Church* (Nashville, TN: Abingdon Press, 1975);

Bernard J. Lee and Michael A. Cowan, *Dangerous Memories: House Churches and Our American Story* (Kansas City, MO: Sheed and Ward, 1986);

C. Kirk Hadaway, Stuart A. Wright, and Francis M. Dubose, *Home Cell Groups and House Churches* (Nashville, TN: Broadman Press, 1987);

Robert Banks, *Paul's Idea of Community: The Early House Churches in Their Historical Setting* (Grand Rapids, MI: William B. Eerdmans Publishing Company and Australia: Anzea Publishers, 1988);

Del Birkey, *The House Church: A Model for Renewing the Church* (Scottdale, PA and Waterloo, Ontario: Herald Press, 1988);

Reta Halteman Finger, *Paul and the Roman House Churches: A Simulation* (Scottdale, PA and Waterloo, Ontario: Herald Press, 1993);

Nate Krupp, *God's Simple Plan for His Church and Your Place in It: A Manual for House Churches,* 2nd ed., (Salem, OR: Preparing the Way Publishers, 1993);

Steve Atkerson, ed., *Toward a House Church Theology* (Atlanta, GA: New Testament Restoration Foundation, 1996);

Carolyn Osiek and David L. Balch, *Families in the New Testament World: Households and House Churches* (Louisville, KY: Westminster John Knox Press, 1997);

Robert and Julia Banks, *The Church Comes Home* (Peabody, MA: Hendrickson Publishers, 1998);

Wolfgang Simpson, *Houses that Change the World: The Return of the House Churches* (UK and Waynesboro, GA: OM Publishing, 1998);

The Fellowship of Church Planters, *Planting House Churches in Networks*, Rev., (Newport, RI: The Fellowship of Church Planters, 1999);

Tom Begier, Tim Richey, Nick Vasiliades, and Frank Viola, *The House Church Movement: Which Direction Will It Take?* (Jacksonville, FL: SeedSowers Christian Books Publishing House, 2001);

Peter Bunton, *Cell Groups and House Churches: What History Teaches Us* (Ephrata, PA: House to House Publications, 2001);

Joseph L. Cartwright, *House Church Planting: Multiplying Colonies of Christ* (Dallas, TX: Dallas Baptist Association House Church Network, 2001);

Robert Fitts, *The Church in the House: A Return to Simplicity* (Salem, OR: Preparing the Way Publishers, 2001);

Larry Kreider, *House Church Networks: A Church for a New Generation* (Ephrata, PA: House to House Publications, 2001);

Felicity Dale, *Getting Started: A Practical Guide to House Church Planting* (n.p.: House2House Ministries, 2002);

Tony and Felicity Dale, *Simply Church* (Austin, TX: Karis Publishing, Inc., 2002);

Frank Viola, *So You Want to Start a House Church: First-Century Styled Church Planting for Today* (n.p.: Present Testimony Ministry, 2003);

William Tenny-Brittian, *House Church Manual* (St. Louis, MO: Chalice Press, 2004);

Roger Gehring, *House Church and Missions: The Importance of Household Structures in Early Christianity* (Peabody, MA: Hendrickson Publishers, Inc, 2004);

Rad Zdero, *The Global House Church Movement* (Pasadena, CA: William Carey Library, 2004);

Carolyn Osiek, Margaret Y. MacDonald, and Janet H. Tulloch, *A Woman's Place: House Churches in Earliest Christianity* (2005);

Larry Kreider and Floyd McClung, *Starting a House Church: A New Model for Living Out Your Faith* (Ventura, CA: Regal, 2007);

Rad Zdero, ed., *Nexus: The World House Church Movement Reader* (Pasadena, CA: William Carey Library, 2007).

2. *Dateline NBC* broadcast December 9, 2005 and *700 Club* broadcast January 16, 2006.

3. *Time* at http://www.time.com/time/magazine/printout/ 0,8816,1167737,00.html (accessed 3/6/06).

4. April Hurst, "Home, Sweet Church: Pastor Holds Services in His Living Room Twice Weekly," *Lexington Herald-Leader,* 18 February 2006, sec. F1.

5. Hannah Elliott, "1 in 5 Adults Attend House Churches, According to First Hard Statistics," Associated Baptist Press, July 6, 2006; http://www.abpnews.com/ www/1198.article.

6. Unless otherwise noted, Scripture references are taken from the Holman Christian Standard Bible.

7. Later, in this Introduction, I will explain why I sometimes use the capitalized form of Church as opposed to church with a lowercase *c*.

8. It is beyond the scope of this book for me to trace the history of churches that have met in homes throughout the centuries. Other proponents of house churches have attempted to show this information. See Rad Zdero, *The Global House Church Movement* (Pasadena, CA: William Carey Library, 2004), 59–69 and Wolfgang Simpson, *Houses that Change the World: The Return of the House Churches* (UK and Waynesboro, GA: OM Publishing, 1998), 57–73.

9. Neil Cole, *Organic Church: Growing Faith Where Life Happens* (San Francisco, CA: Jossey-Bass, 2005), xxix.

10. For those interested in our research methods, see appendix 1.

11. George Barna, *Revolution* (Wheaton, IL: Tyndale House Publishers, 2005), 65.

12. For example, Eph. 1:22 and Phil. 3:6 both obviously refer to something larger than the church in one particular location. Also, 1 Cor. 16:1, 2 Cor. 8:1, and 2 Thess. 1:4 clearly refer to local expressions of the body of Christ.

13. For example, in September 2004, Stan Norman, a theology professor at the New Orleans Baptist Theological Seminary wrote a paper for the North American Mission Board entitled "Ecclesiological Guidelines to Inform Southern Baptist Church Planters"; also the International Mission Board has a shorter but similar paper. Both of these are outstanding documents that I wholeheartedly endorse. Norman's document can be located at www.churchplantingvillage.com. For a condensed understanding of my ecclesiology see Section VI (The Church) of the Baptist Faith and Message 2000 at http://www.sbc.net/bfm/bfm2000.asp.

14. There has been much discussion surrounding the *missional* church in recent years. It is beyond the scope of this book to address this concept in detail. For additional information on the history and a contemporary understanding of the discussion, see Darrell L. Guder, ed., *Missional Church: A Vision for the Sending of the Church in North America* (Grand Rapids, MI: William B. Eerdmans, 1998), or visit the Gospel and Our Culture Network at www.gocn.org.

15. Thom S. Rainer, "A Resurgence Not Yet Realized: Evangelistic Effectiveness in the Southern Baptist Convention Since 1979," *The Southern Baptist Journal of Theology* 9 (Spring 2005); 64.

16. Steve Atkerson, ed., *Toward a House Church Theology* (Atlanta, GA: New Testament Restoration Foundation, 1996), Introduction.

17. Many of the churches in our study would also be comfortable describing themselves with terms such as *simple, organic,* and/or *relational.*

18. Wolfgang Simpson, *Houses That Change the World: The Return of the House Churches* (UK: OM Publishing, 1998), xxx–xxxi.

19. Jack Redford, *Planting New Churches* (Nashville, TN: Broadman Press, 1978), 64.

20. Larry Kreider, *House Church Networks: A Church for a New Generation* (Ephrata, PA: House to House Publishers, 2001), 31.

21. Laurie Goodstein, "Search for the Right Churches Ends at Home," *The New York Times*, Late Edition (April 29, 2001), Section 1, pg. 1.

22. Rad Zdero, *The Global House Church Movement* (Pasadena, CA: William Carey Library, 2004), 74–75.

23. Rita Healy and David Van Biema, "Why Home Churches Are Filling Up," *Time*, online (February 27, 2006); http://www.time.com/time/magazine/article/0,9171,1167737-1,00.html (accessed 3/6/06).

24. For more information on the research methodology and limitations of our study, please see appendix 1.

Chapter 1: What Is the C/church Anyway?

1. Matthew 16:18.

2. http://www.quotationspage.com/quote/24312.html (accessed 8/26/05).

3. *New American Standard Updated Edition Exhaustive Concordance of the Bible with Hebrew-Aramaic and Greek Dictionaries* (La Habra, CA: The Lockman Foundation, 1981), Greek NASB number: 1577.

4. Also, there is no 2 Hezekiah 3:16. I just wanted to make this clear before I start receiving nasty e-mails.

5. http://www.m-w.com (accessed 07/13/07).

6. Starting with the Gospels in no way negates Old Testament theology. In fact, without a proper understanding of the Old Testament, it is difficult to understand fully the New Testament. For the sake of space, I am prevented from developing an Old Testament theology leading up to the birth of the Church.

7. Of course, I was referring to her beauty in this illustration! Again, I want to avoid nasty e-mails.

8. For a discussion of this matter see Jonathan S. Campbell, "The Translatability of Christian Community: An Ecclesiology for Postmodern Cultures and Beyond," Ph.D. Dissertation, Fuller Theological Seminary, 1999. Though I am not in agreement with all of his assumptions and conclusions, Campbell's arguments have influenced this section.

9. http://www.house2house.net/modules.php?name=FAQ&myfaq=yes&id_cat=1&cate-gories=Simple+Church+Basics (accessed 9/1/05).

10. Nate Krupp, "A Growing House Church Movement"; Accessed at http://www.cellchurch.info/ Articles/Nate%20Krupp/A%20Growing%20House%20-Church%20Movement.htm (accessed 9/2/05).

11. Tony and Felicity Dale, *Simply Church* (Austin, TX: Karis Publishing, Inc., 1996); Robert Fitts, *The Church in the House: A Return to Simplicity* (Salem, OR: Preparing the Way Publishers, 2001); and Nate Krupp, *God's Simple Plan for His Church and Your Place in It: A Manual for House Churches*, 2nd edition (Salem, OR: Preparing the Way Publishers, 1993).

12. For example, see Neil Cole, "Out of Control Order: Simple Structures for a Decentralized Multiplication Movement"; http://www.cmaresources.com/articles/sim-ple_structures.asp (accessed 2/8/06).

13. Rusty Entrekin, "When You Come Together," *Toward A House Church Theology*, ed. Steve Atkerson (Atlanta, GA: New Testament Restoration Foundation, 1996), 11. Entrekin's comments raise an interesting, yet concerning, issue regarding pastors, a topic I will address in a later chapter.

14. http://www.house2house.net/modules.php?name=FAQ&myfaq=yes &id_cat=1&cate-gories=Sim-ple+Church+Basics#4 (accessed 9/2/05).

CHAPTER 2: MEET THE MISSIONAL HOUSE CHURCHES

1. It is likely that the percentages provided by the leaders are rough estimates. Questions about ethnicity were asked over the telephone, requiring the participant to draw from memory the ethnic diversity among the churches. Though there is much room for error with such reporting, it is clear that these churches had a great amount of ethnic diversity.

2. Larry Kreider, *House Church Networks: A Church for a New Generation* (Ephrata, PA: House to House Publications, 2001).

3. Lyle Schaller, "What is Your Definition of Small," *Circuit Rider* (November/December 2001); 24; http://www.umph.com/pdfs/circuitrider/6618YDoS.pdf (accessed 3/7/06).

4. See http://www.smallchurch.com (accessed 3/7/06).

5. Carl S. Dudley and David A. Roozen, "Faith Communities Today: A Report on Religion in the United States Today" (The Hartford Institute for Religion Research, Hartford Seminary, March 2001), 8; http://fact.hartsem.edu/Final%20FACTrpt.pdf (accessed 3/7/06).

6. George Barna, *Revolution* (Wheaton, IL: Tyndale House Publishers, 2005), 29.

7. Eddie Gibbs and Ryan K. Bolgner, *Emerging Churches: Creating Christian Community in Postmodern Cultures* (Grand Rapids, MI: Baker Academic, 2005), 145.

8. This assumption was based on the speculation that house churches would have very short life spans. Though more research needs to be done regarding the lifecycles of North American house churches, I was surprised that over half of the churches in our study were older than three years of age.

9. Granted, it should be noted that it is possible isolationists were not fairly represented in our sample because they would be the very ones who would not participate in an online survey.

10. Only twenty-two of the thirty-three churches are represented here because eleven leaders did not respond or responded in unusual ways that could not be coded for this research.

CHAPTER 3: CHURCH GROWTH AND MISSIONAL HOUSE CHURCHES

1. Acts 6:7.

2. George Barna, "Surveys Show Pastors Claim Congregants Are Deeply Committed to God But Congregants Deny It," January 10, 2006; www.barna.org (accessed 2/27/06).

3. Roger W. Gehring, *House Church and Mission: The Importance of Household Structures in Early Christianity* (Peabody, MA: Hendrickson Publishers, 2004), 309.

4. Thom S. Rainer, *The Book of Church Growth: History, Theology, and Principles* (Nashville, TN: Broadman and Holman Publishers, 1993), 23.

5. See Donald A. McGavran, *Understanding Church Growth* (Grand Rapids, MI: William B. Eerdmans Publishing Company, 1970).

6. LifeWay Christian Resources is located in Nashville, Tennessee and is affiliated with the Southern Baptist Convention.

7. Thom S. Rainer, "First-Person: LifeWay Research: Lighting a Path," *Baptist Press News,* February 21, 2006; http://www.bpnews.net/bpnews.asp?ID=22700 (accessed 2/21/06).

8. Thom S. Rainer, "A Resurgence Not Yet Realized: Evangelistic Effectiveness in the Southern Baptist Convention Since 1979," *The Southern Baptist Journal of Theology* 9 (Spring 2005): 64.

9. Ibid.

10. For example, certain people are baptized but are not followers of Christ. Sometimes people are re-baptized but were obviously converted one time. Sometimes children are baptized but have yet to place their faith in Christ for salvation.

11. Chris Turner, "Rainer Calls for Boldness in a Spiritually Hungry World," *Baptist Press News*, February 9, 2006; http://www.bpnews.net/bpnews.asp?ID=22621 (accessed 2/15/06).

12. Sometimes church growth researchers recommend comparing worship attendance rather than actual church membership.

13. This percentage is determined by taking the average number of annual baptisms (4–6) and dividing it by the average size of the house churches (14–17) and multiplying the number by 100.

14. This is a generalization. There are many older traditional churches in North America that would be statistically evangelistically effective. See Thom Rainer, *Effective Evangelistic Churches* (Nashville, TN: Broadman and Holman Publishers, 1996).

15. We actually had seven participants to report their churches had been meeting for ten or more years. One of the surveys failed to show the size range of the church making the item uncodeable. Because of this lack of data, I have only listed these six churches.

16. McGavran, 63.

17. Peter Wagner, *Church Planting for a Greater Harvest* (Ventura, CA: Regal Books, 1990), 11.

18. One potential weakness in our study was that a definition of "church" was not given. Like most church growth researchers to date, I assumed a common understanding. To my knowledge, no researcher has ever presented a definition of church when asking church leaders to reveal information about their congregations.

19. The initial survey comprised Phase I of our research. See appendix 2.

20. We could not code 9 percent of the responses, hence the reason the percentages do not add up to 100 percent.

21. Concerning strangers or "person X," see W. Oscar Thompson, Jr., *Concentric Circles of Concern* (Nashville, TN: Broadman Press, 1981).

22. Robert and Julia Banks, *The Church Comes Home* (Peabody, MA: Hendrickson Publishers, 1998), 233.

23. I suspect that more of the churches are using an invitation to church activities plus relationships than was reported. Sometimes I wondered if many of the participants were actually thinking that their churches were using invitations plus relationships, but they only allowed the relational aspect to be reported. A better survey tool would be helpful for future research.

24. Additional future research questions should include: "Since most of the churches in the study were small in number but had been reaching a large percentage of their members through evangelism, were these new believers being sent out to plant other churches, remaining with the original church, failing to be assimilated, etc.?" "Were these missional house churches intentionally remaining small while they carried out the Great Commission?"

25. Thom S. Rainer, *High Expectations: The Remarkable Secret for Keeping People in Your Church* (Nashville, TN: Broadman and Holman Publishers, 1999), 45.

26. Thom S. Rainer, *Effective Evangelistic Churches: Successful Church Reveal What Works and What Doesn't* (Nashville, TN: Broadman and Holman Publishers, 1996), 173.

27. Here is a clear example of the fact that churches without pastors/ elders should not remain for long in such a state.

28. Rad Zdero, *The Global House Church Movement* (Pasadena, CA: William Carey Publishers, 2004), 100.

29. Robert E. Logan and Neil Cole, *Raising Leaders for the Harvest* (St. Charles, IL: Church Smart Resources, 1992–95).

30. Robert E. Coleman, *The Master Plan of Evangelism*, 30th Anniversary ed. (Grand Rapids, MI: Fleming H. Revell, 1993).

CHAPTER 4: MONEY AND MISSIONAL HOUSE CHURCHES

1. See Jim Melon, "The Big Bang (For Your Bucks) Theory"; http://www. house2house.net/ modules.php?name=News&file=article&sid=162 (accessed 2/10/06).

2. Rad Zdero, *The Global House Church Movement* (Pasadena, CA: William Carey Library 2004), 140.

3. John White, "Financing Ministry," *House2House* 6: 21.

4. Ibid.

5. Steve Atkerson, *Toward a House Church Theology* (Atlanta, GA: New Testament Restoration Foundation, 1998), 82–83.

6. Cole understands contemporary apostles as missionaries or church planters.

7. Neil Cole, "Financing the Work," *House2House* 6: 17–19.

8. Ibid., 19.

9. E. E. Carpenter, "Tithe," *International Standard Bible Encyclopedia*, fully revised, ed. Geoffrey W. Bromiley (Wm. B. Eerdmans, 1988), 862.

10. Ibid.

11. I realize there are several definitions of *tentmaker*, but I believe that this one comes closest to the biblical description of a tentmaker.

12. J. Christy Wilson, Jr., *Today's Tentmakers: Self-support: An Alternative Model for Worldwide Witness* (Wheaton, IL: Tyndale House Publishers, 1979), 16. For an excellent contemporary work see Patrick Lai, *Tentmaking: Business as Missions* (Waynesboro, GA: Authentic Media, 2005).

13. "We are fools for Christ, but you are wise in Christ! We are weak, but you are strong! You are distinguished, but we are dishonored! Up to the present hour we are both hungry and thirsty; we are poorly clothed, roughly treated, homeless; we labor, working with our own hands. When we are reviled, we bless; when we are persecuted, we endure it; when we are slandered, we entreat. We are, even now, like the world's garbage, like the filth of all things" (1 Cor. 4:10–13).

14. 2 Thess. 3:6–12.

15. Dick Scoggins, *Building Effective Church Planting Teams* (Middletown, RI: Fellowship of Church Planters, n.d.), 37–38.

16. F. F. Bruce, *Paul: Apostle of the Heart Set Free* (Grand Rapids, MI: Wm. B. Eerdmans, 1977), 220.

CHAPTER 5: THE FUTURE OF MISSIONAL HOUSE CHURCHES

1. http://www.goodquotes.com/famouslastwords.htm (accessed 8/19/05).

2. Despite his comment, it should be noted that there were some influential cell churches on the eastern side of the country, including some megacell churches.

3. It should be noted that these two examples are not the first people involved in house church life in the United States. In our research, we had other participants inform us that they had been involved in house churches since the 1970s.

4. http://www.dba.net/church_planting_models.asp (accessed 9/1/05), emphasis mine.

5. Larry Kreider, *House Church Networks: A Church for a New Generation* (Ephrata, PA: House to House Publications, 2001), 89.

6. Ibid.

7. I realize that some folks in house churches do not have or desire an official membership, but I could not bring myself to refer to these people as "participants." For the believer, membership in the body of Christ is not optional at either the universal or local level (1 Cor. 12) but a part of both our being and obedience.

8. See chapter 3.

9. Andrew Jones, "My Gripes about the House Church Movement"; http://www.theooze.com/articles/ print.cfm?id=291&page=1 (accessed 2/21/06).

10. http://www.quoteland.com/topic.asp?CATEGORY_ID=186 (accessed 9/2/05).

11. The five most critical issues facing North American church planters in order of most critical to least critical were 1) money, 2) leadership development, 3) apathetic or turfish churches, 4) contextualization of the gospel, and 5) family pressures.

12. Rad Zdero, *The Global House Church Movement* (Pasadena, CA: William Carey Library, 2004), 14.

CHAPTER 6: CHURCH PLANTING MOVEMENTS AND MISSIONAL HOUSE CHURCHES

1. Roland Allen, *The Spontaneous Expansion of the Church: And the Causes Which Hinder It* (Grand Rapids, MI: Eerdmans, 1962), 156.

2. Donald A. McGavran, *Understanding Church Growth* (Grand Rapids, MI: Eerdmans, 1970), 62–63.

3. 2 Thess. 3:1.

4. For those of you who are wondering, *The Andy Griffith Show* is the other all-time greatest television program.

5. Allen, *Spontaneous,* 7.

6. For an academic treatment of this topic, see Jervis D. Payne, "An Evaluation of the Systems Approach to North American Church Multiplication Movements of Robert E. Logan in Light of the Missiology of Roland Allen," Ph.D. dissertation, The Southern Baptist Theological Seminary 2001, 16–98.

7. David Garrison, *Church Planting Movements: How God is Redeeming a Lost World* (Midlothian, VA: WIGTake Resources, 2004), 21. See appendix 4 for a list of characteristics found in all church planting movements.

8. Not that there is anything wrong with jeans or Hawaiian shirts.

9. Garrison, 192–93.

10. Taken from www.imb.org/cpm/Chapter7.htm (accessed 3/1/06).

11. Ibid.

12. John 3:8.

13. Isaiah 55:8.

14. Adolf Harnack, *The Expansion of Christianity in the First Three Centuries,* vol. 1, trans. James Moffatt, (New York: Books for Libraries Press, 1904–05, reprint 1972), 397.

15. Tom A. Steffen, *Passing the Baton* (La Habra, CA: Center for Organization and Ministry, 1997).

16. David Garrison, *Church Planting Movements* (Richmond, VA: IMB, 2000). A free copy of the booklet can be ordered from http://www.imb. org/cpm (accessed 2/28/06). There is also an excellent corresponding twelve-minute video produced under the same title. For more information, contact International Mission Board Resource Center, 800-866-3621, product number: DM-01102.

17. Garrison, 155.

18. Ibid., 156.

19. Ibid., 156.

20. Ibid., 157.

21. Ibid., 159.

22. Ibid., 161.

23. Ibid., 168.

24. Ibid.

25. Ibid., 271.

26. Ibid., 301.

APPENDIX 4: COMMON CHARACTERISTICS OF EVERY CHURCH PLANTING MOVEMENT

1. Taken from David Garrison, *Church Planting Movements: How God Is Redeeming a Lost World* (Midlothian, VA: WIGTake Resources, 2004), 172.

APPENDIX 5: CHARACTERISTICS OF MOST CHURCH PLANTING MOVEMENTS

1. Taken from David Garrison, *Church Planting Movements: How God Is Redeeming a Lost World* (Midlothian, VA: WIGTake Resources, 2004), 221–22.